And This Is How I Lived

stories from overlanders, immigrants, settlers,
and pioneers who made new lives in difficult places

Carolyn Wing Greenlee

And This Is How I Lived

stories of overlanders, immigrants, settlers, and pioneers
who made new lives in difficult places

© Copyright 2018 Carolyn Wing Greenlee
Written and collected by Carolyn Wing Greenlee
Cover design: Stephanie Del Bosco and Dan Worley
Divider pages: Stephanie C Del Bosco
Layout: Dan Worley

Photos courtesy of Loretta Burriss Ussery,
the Andrew Rocca family, Carolyn Wing Greenlee

ISBN
978-1-887400-55-8 (paperback)

Earthen Vessel Productions
www.earthen.com

ACKNOWLEDGMENTS

Special thanks to Bart and Roy Rocca, who supplied photos and information, and who made it possible for me to reprint some of the most significant stories in the historical record through the writings of Helen Rocca Goss, daughter of their great great grandfather, Andrew Rocca.

Many thanks to Donna Howard (retired curator of Lakeport Museum in Lake County, California) and Theresa Hanley (retired director of the Ontario Museum of History and Art, Ontario, California) who significantly changed the course of my life with their enthusiasm for history, their readiness to host events for me at their venues, and the connections they facilitated that became life-long friendships that influenced and blessed yet more lives down the line.

Thank you to fifth generation Lake County resident Wilda Shock, whose energy, generosity, and kindness have powered many an educational opportunity that has enriched the communities she serves so diligently.

And to J. Clark McAbee, Curator of the Lake County museums, who loves story and is creating innovative ways of preserving the voices and faces of the people here, our treasures of living history.

Front cover photos
(left to right)
Top: Lewis Chamblee Borroughs with daughter Francis Henrietta,
Hulda Bagley, Andrew Rocca
Middle: Letty and sister Elva, Thomas W. Wing, Kathleen Kong Wing
Bottom: Margaret Ann Wright, the children of Andrew Rocca

Back cover photos
Excursion on Clear Lake, 1892.
Far left in the black hat is Martha Mitchell Burriss, Letty's
paternal grandmother

Gong family photo
(left to right)
Back row: Bill, Hong Chee (Pop), Wong Shee (Mom), Kathleen
Front row: Walter, Marilyn, Katie

CONTENTS

Foreword

Carolyn Wing Greenlee has selected a beautiful literary bouquet of local history and heritage concerning Lake County and beyond. In these intriguing and insightful stories the lives of ordinary people become extraordinary. From the journey of fourteen year old boy/man Joseph N. Borroughs along the Oregon Trail to the soul-crushing first steps of a four year old Chinese girl sold into slavery by her famine stricken parents. Taken by a stranger across the vast Pacific Ocean to Gum San, Gold Mountain-California. Despite this unimaginably difficult beginning to her life Chun Shee overcame it all to become a successful, graceful and respected lady in society.

These powerful memoirs and more tell of the triumphs and tragedies of the human spirit in our corner of the world. At their essence they are uniquely American stories and remind us that we each live and create our own history every day. Carolyn Wing Greenlee thankfully sought out these captivating tales for *This Is How I Lived* blending in her own experiences and story. The result is a book that inspires hope, highlights not only our frailties and our successes but ultimately affirms our shared humanity regardless of color, creed or social standing. It is both a rough and tumble yet elegantly entertaining and enlightening read.

J. Clark McAbee, Curator
Museums of Lake County

INTRODUCTION

Where are your people from? Mine came from the east, the Far East, enduring a miserably seasick month in steerage to debark onto the soil of *Gum San*, Gold Mountain, in the hope of making a better life for their families. Many others came from the other east for the same reason—or for adventure or to start a new and different kind of life. California in those days had few laws and individuals could establish themselves in a place where opportunities were vast and needs were many. So were the hardships, hazards, and dangers. Interestingly, the Chinese word for crisis is a combination of two other words: danger and opportunity.

I have long been curious about what caused people to go to so much trouble to get here, and how they managed to survive and even flourish once they did. I retraced the California/Oregon Trail, walking in ruts of wagon wheels still deeply carved in rocky places a century or so after the last overlanders trekked the long way with covered wagons. They were called go-backers if they turned around, and pioneers if they stayed. What made them stay?

And This Is How I Lived is a collection of stories from some of the books Earthen Vessel has been involved with over the past twenty-five years. At the start of each section, I've explained how the books came about. And here and there are a few of my poems. Feel free to skip whatever is not your cup of tea, or read start to finish if you want to experience the entire journey.

Of the many stories I've encountered in my research, writing, and publishing, certain ones have remained fresh in my mind. Some are quirky, some funny, some surprising, tender, terrible, thought-provoking, or purely entertaining. In this juxtaposition of human lives that left their legacy on this land, one thing is clear: each person's existence has made a difference that continues to flow through generations in the unique heritage that was made possible because they came—and stayed.

—Carolyn Wing Greenlee
Kelseyville, CA

for Dan
for twenty-five years of creative partnership
bringing into being
far more than I ever thought possible.
You are a true pioneer.

Journey With
The Wagon Master

Joseph Newton Borroughs
1840-1919

Journey With The Wagon Master

Journey With The Wagon Master
By Joseph Newton Borroughs

INTRODUCTION

I was lousy at history, but I loved museums. To me, the items in the cases were not artifacts of irrelevant past, but evidence that those people really lived and these were things they made from their need, their ingenuity, and their environments. Their stories were even more intriguing because they shared their thoughts as well as the details of their days. I particularly liked primary documents written by those who had lived those events and given them feelings and observations. I loved their voices, their inflections of thought and speech almost as different from ours as another dialect in Chinese. Interestingly, many accounts were the experiences of children, written by them later as mature adults recounting memories, giving them significance and meaning from the perspective of many years. It pained me to know that quite a few of these old books had gone out of print. That was one of the main reasons I started my own publishing company. I decided that nothing Earthen Vessel ever published would go out of print.

One day Donna Howard, Curator of the Lake County Museum, asked if I would consider republishing some books of local history that were no longer available. Of course I said yes. That is how I met sixth generation Lake County resident Loretta Burriss Ussery.

Letty was in her eighties when my assistant Stephanie Boyette and I met her, a dauntless traveler, a painter of respectable reputation, and an adventurer loaded with the strength, energy, and endurance of her forefathers. In 1849 her great grandfather Lewis Chamblee Borroughs had taken a 440 acre land grant in Scotts Valley in Lake County, California. Seven generations of the family made it their home. It was in the house her great grandfather built that we met with Letty—often and so delightfully that we became good friends.

One day while we were sitting visiting at her kitchen table, Letty mentioned she had an unpublished manuscript that her great uncle Joseph had written fifty years after he made the trip from South Carolina to California with his brother Lewis, the wagon master. She asked if I would be interested in publishing it. Of course I said yes.

We found Joseph's account charming—unhurried and sometimes whimsical in the style of an expert storyteller of that era. We changed none of the text, preserving even the punctuation to maintain its authenticity and flavor. Since the memoir had no title, I named the book "Journey With The Wagon Master."

I want to add that I was afraid the Oregon/California Trail Association (OCTA) would tell me they already had more than enough books of overlanders' trips and did not want to bother with even one more. Standing in their bookstore looking at the crowded shelves, I voiced my concerns to Director Kathy Conway. She stunned me by saying people were always coming in looking through books for the names of relatives that might be mentioned in a diary, journal, or memoir. Overlanders stopped at different and encountered different people. "Every trip is different," she told me. "Every voice is important." And she ordered copies of our book for their store. Later I received a letter from OCTA verifying the authenticity of the memoir. I was thrilled. We had preserved and made visible another treasure of the trail, a contribution to family heritage, public enrichment, and the historical record.

You may not see anything worth retelling of your own trek to where you are now, but perhaps as you review the events that turned your path this way or the other, you will remember something worth sharing of how you faced your adversities. Do not disregard your own successes, for every time you chose not to go back, you won a victory. Your family will be enriched by the telling because your journey is unique, everything you learned has value, and your voice is important. Your life matters. So do your stories.

"How would you like to go to California with Lewis?"

These were the words addressed to me, by an older, motherly sister one morning as I sat by the fireside in my father's home.

I was then a boy in my fourteenth year. Lewis was an older brother, a man doing for himself before the days of my first recollection.

This, however, is not to be a family history; but a reminiscent account of my trip to California. The remark of my sister was the first intimation I had that any one but myself ever thought of such a thing as my going to California. Brother Lewis had already made three trips across the "Great American Desert", as it was then called; the first one being in 1849. I also had another brother, James, far west, California, by water, but who died of cholera almost upon his arrival. But ever after I had an unceasing desire, and fully intended at some future time to see the Golden State, though had never mentioned it to my most intimate friends.

But when sister Eliza put the question above to me, a suspicion arose in my mind that, somehow, the question of my going with Lewis was being discussed in the family, and my reply was:

"O I wish I could!"

Then began the most earnest persuasion of her mind and heart against my thinking even of such a thing. All the difficulties, dangers, trials and possible sufferings of the journey, together with what then seemed an almost endless distance, by which I would be separated from all the other members of the family; also the almost certain and near-heartbreaking homesickness with which I would be attacked; together with every other argument she could think of, was brought to bear upon me. However, the old saying of "water on a duck's back" would have been very applicable, so far as the effect in restraining my desire to undertake the journey went. Indeed, to use another of like classical character, it "added fuel to the fire."

I found out, though, from her, that the subject of my going was under consideration by my Father and brother. This, of course, doubled, if possible, my boyish desire to cross the plains, see the sights on the way and on the west coast of our great country. The pleadings of my sisters were continued from time to time, even up to the morning of our departure, which was the 7th of September, 1854.

I wish here to serve timely notice that my leaving my home was in no sense because it was not a good home. As I sit today writing, and think, as I have doubtless a thousand times before, I cannot recall a single element that was wanting to make mine a perfectly pleasant, and desirable home in every particular. I do most certainly think no boy ever entertained more profound respect and love for his father than I did for mine, poorly as I may have shown it, and as much as I may now regret my failure to have done so.

No, it was just my boyish, and in some respects thoughtless desires to ramble and satisfy my curiosity to see and know what was beyond the bounds of my home life. And this, as with all other boys in those days and that country, was quite limited.

That seventh of September morning will, I think, be among the last things fading from my memory. I had seen my beloved Father stand beside the death bed of a dear sister of mine, and never a tear dimmed his eyes, and I wondered with great childish wonder why, when everybody else was weeping bitterly. I learned later why, by hearing him say to some friends, that the great sorrow of his life was that he could not find relief for an over burdened heart in tears, like other people.

But on that September morn, when he came to take the parting hand with his baby boy, there were tears in his eyes and upon his cheeks; and it required all my boyish desires for travel and sight seeing in strong exercise, to prevent my getting off my horse and refusing to go. I had somehow managed to say good-bye to the other members of the family, my stepmother and sisters, each of whom I loved with all my boyish affection, with a fair degree of courage, but this was my Waterloo. I could hide my tears no longer, and wept freely, somewhat, at least, to the relief of a burdened heart.

But we were off, and soon, with new sights, and a boy's native talent for throwing off trouble, my sorrow soon passed away. For was I not really on the road to California, and were there not before me the great plains and mountains and Indians and what not to be seen and known? Surely mine were great opportunities.

So in the space of about twelve miles, we crossed the river, at that point the dividing line between my native state of South Carolina, and Georgia; and I was on entirely new territory. And already I began to feel quite the traveler for one of my age, which wanted from that time to the twenty-fifth of December to carry me to my fifteenth year.

Unlikely Companions

On the fourth day we renewed our journey; brother and his partner buying cattle where they found a cheap lot for sale, in Alabama, Mississippi, Tennessee and Kentucky, gathering about three hundred head.

We crossed the Mississippi at Mills Point, ferrying the cattle over, I suppose about forty at a load. Lewis and I went over with the first load, and Mat., remained to herd those left behind. After getting the first load off the boat, Lewis returned with the boat, and I herded those taken over.

It was seemingly almost human, the interest manifested on the part of those cattle to return to those left on the other side. And at times it was quite a little trouble to keep some of them from taking the water in an effort to swim back.

While heading off some that were making for the river, a white dog came to my assistance, and soon put a stop to their efforts along this line.

Whether this dog had become lost from some former drover crossing there, we never knew, but he most persistently refused to be separated from us after that, and followed us the rest of the afternoon and remained over night when we ceased trying to scold

7

him back. By accident, or otherwise, the majority of his caudal appendage had been amputated, so we named him Bob. Whether he had known the name formerly or not, he seemed to take a fancy to it, and Bob he was all the way to California, and quite a helpful Bob, too, on many occasions.

While driving in the Mississippi bottoms, which we did for some days, we were passing occasional farm houses and small lots of stock, hogs, cattle, etc.

A little after noon one day, we noticed a pig, weighing perhaps forty or fifty pounds, going along with the cattle, and I was deputized to drive it from among them. I did so and kept it to one side and held it back till the hindmost cattle had passed, when I took my place in driving the cattle. But in short order Mr. Pig was again seen with the drove. Again I was put in commission, and this time drove it back the road a hundred or more yards. But this young porker seemed to think he had as much right to take a journey as other cattle. No sooner would I cease my efforts to drive him back than he would renew his efforts to return to the drove.

Finally I gave him a big boost toward his supposed home, and turned my horse and trotted briskly to the drove. It was not long till we discovered that piggy had played us the same trick the man did the fifty Indians, when fighting them single handed; he had surrounded us and was up near the front of the line. I tried the same game on him some more; but that pig sure must have thought he had been born somewhere out west, and wanted to get back home, for when we camped that night (we had a wagon and camping outfit now) he was promptly on hand, chirk and cheery as you please.

We wanted to leave him with the farmer where we camped and fed our cattle, but he said not so, as it was not his pig, and as he had so persistently stayed with us for half a day, we should just let him alone till he stopped of his own accord. He was up bright and fresh next morning and ready for an early start. As he had met with the same misfortune as our dog and, as we already had one Bob, we dubbed him stiff tail, and Stiff Tail he was to the end. ...But I think that pig was a Missourian, for he was never satisfied till we made a halt in that state. Either that or he must have concluded he was a cow, for he stayed with them while he lived.

... Just here I am reminded that I owe Stiff Tail an apology, as he was an Arkansan instead of a Mississippian, for it was in the Black River, and not the Mississippi River, Bottoms, that he fell in love with us. It would never do to mix or misplace his pigship with any other stock or locality. In proof of which I offer the following fact, here for the first time made historical, in evidence.

After a few days' travel he became foot sore and leg weary, and I caught him and put him in the wagon, which I was driving them.

Of course, as any other intelligent swine would have done, he made somewhat strenuous objection, but climbing in with him and holding him until he became convinced what it all meant, he soon grew reconciled to his new experience as to the method of travel, laid himself down and rested contentedly. After a time he showed signs of having a desire to foot it again, and I put him out.

Ever after this, when he got tired, he would come up from the rear end of the cattle where he generally traveled and would come as near asking for a ride as any pig I ever listened to. And he always got it.

Little Black River

In the spring when the mountain snow melts, Black River (this one called Little Black, as there are two of them) is not small by any means. When the snows are abundant in the mountains, the river backs its waters into all the sloughs, which are quite numerous on both sides of the river. Hence almost all that region of country is overflowed. There is no damage resulting, however, in that part, for as previously said, the land lies low. The River itself has but little fall, and the flood waters are all, or nearly all, back water with but little current.

...The water at our camp became sufficiently warmed to be pleasant for bathing. One day I concluded to have a bath. I was no expert swimmer, but could paddle around fairly well.

After being in the water for a time, I concluded to swim across the river, which was, at this time, about thirty or forty yards in width. I swam across quite handily and climbed out on the bank. After sitting there for a time, I began to dread the return trip; in fact, became somewhat afraid to undertake it. I knew if I called for any one to bring the canoe over for me, the boys would laugh at me for being cowardly.

Of the two things, I dreaded more to be called a coward than to tackle the swim. So I plunged in and started out pretty well. But the further I went the more frightened I became, and soon found myself kicking and pawing for dear life. And kick and paw was all I was doing, excepting to drift down the current, for I was about half way across. Seeing my frantic efforts were accomplishing nothing but my exhaustion, I mentally said this, or felt it, if you chose to put it that way: "If I am going to drown, I'll do it just as easily as anybody on earth can." Immediately upon this conclusion, I started out and swam with as much or more ease to myself than ever, either before or since.

I really think this was the best lesson in the way of self control I ever had. For surely had I continued my useless exertions, I soon would have been exhausted and have drowned. Many persons lose their lives simply from want of self control. And not only in like circumstances, but under such as may be quite different.

WOLVES

Brother and his partner decided to drive into winter quarters on Little Black River in Arkansas, which we reached somewhere about the 20th of October. ...Driving up the river about three miles, a place immediately on the banks of the stream was chosen as the location for our camp, after two or three days' inspection of the surrounding country. We were about forty miles south, or perhaps west of south slightly, from Poplar Bluffs, and our camp was built, as nearly as known, exactly on the line between Arkansas and Missouri. So we slept in one state and ate in the other, thinking a change of locality might be good.

…The fourth day after our arrival, Mat. took Lewis to the Mississippi River where he (Lewis) took boat for Saint Louis, Missouri, to arrange supplies for our trip across the plains. Wagons were to be built for the purpose, ox yokes, chains, etc., with tents, bedding and whatever was necessary. Having made the journey three times before, he well understood how to make all necessary arrangements for it.

I was left, of course, to look after camp affairs, with Bob for a companion, and a lonely time we two had for four days, the time Mat. was gone. At night, however, it was different. These swamps, or bottom lands (for they were not marshy) were infested with the large grey or timber wolves. They not only could, but did, make night hideous, to me, at least, with their howling. One could make seemingly as much, and as many different kinds of noise, as would a dozen dogs howling at the same time.

I was told to sleep in the wagon and to take Bob in with me. The cover to the wagon was made of good, strong sail canvas, and could be well fastened down at the sides with strong leather straps and buckles at the sides; and at the ends were large open seams, through which were put light strong cords and by these the ends of this cover could be drawn together, thus completely closing it, so that nothing could get out or in.

Well, you may be sure I made everything as secure as straps and cords could make them, and Bob and I turned in for the night, he lying close to my feet. I was just beginning to feel dozy when, in the distance, I heard, as it seemed to me, half a dozen different and most hideous noises at the same time, ending finally with one long, lonesome, doleful howl. Being the first of the kind I ever heard, I could not, of course, know what it was. But I was not left to guess a great while, for scarcely had the first ceased, before in another direction the first was repeated and then still another somewhere else, until it seemed the whole woods were filled with them. To make bad matters worse, for I assure you they were already bad enough, I found from all directions they seemed to be coming for the camp. I felt that I was in no danger as they could not get to me if they desired, and I had a good doublebarrelled shot gun, and both barrels loaded, besides Bob. But that dog made me more trouble than the wolves, for he seemed determined to get out, and have some sort of a mix up with them, for they were soon around the wagon. I felt certain that the mix would not be favorable to Bob, so, while I was quite sure he could not get out, to make assurance doubly sure, I took a small rope and tied it around his neck and tied each end to a bow of the wagon cover, thus securing him about midway of the wagon. The wolves not being satisfied with what they soon found was a failure, so far as the contents of the wagon were concerned began a fight among themselves.

Now, you may think I felt no interest in their amusement among themselves, but I did. For, first of all, there was no bone of contention among them, so far as I could see, and I was positive there was none from camp cooking, as we only had bacon in the wagon and there were no bones in it. But they fought just the same. And I am not able even at this late date to tell which was the more anxious to see that fight, the boy or the dog that was in the wagon. I talked to Bob and tried to persuade him to keep quiet, as it was not his fight, and he replied in his own way, but whether he was trying to persuade me to not peep under the edges of the wagon cover and look at what he was not permitted to see, I never could find out.

As to the outcome of that fight or its general order, if there was any order to it, I knew nothing, for I could see nothing. I felt very much, though, as the old lady expressed herself when she saw her husband and a bear fighting, and said she never saw a fight in her life in which she felt so little interest as to who won.

I suppose they got all they wanted of it, and perhaps some of them more, for they quit, whether they were satisfied, all hands around, with results or not. Anyhow, we in the wagon were glad when they left, at least, I was, and as I heard nothing to the contrary from Bob, I supposed he was also.

As nothing occurred to disturb us the remainder of the night, boy and dog alike, we slept quite soundly until morning.

About two hundred yards from our wagon was a log cabin, built by some parties who were getting out stave timber to ship to New Orleans the next spring. This was oak trees sawed into blocks six feet long and split into pieces of size and shape ready to be dressed into staves for making large tubs or barrels, etc.

These men's homes were on Crowley's Ridge about twenty miles East at the eastern edge of the swamp, and they were at their homes for some two weeks at this time. I took possession of that cabin next day, and had Bob and myself shut in and the wolves out when night came on, for they came earlier, were more numerous, stayed later and fought worse than the night before.

I suppose, though, they made final settlement of their troubles, or concluded the proceeds from camp supplies didn't pay for their serenade and tragical performance both, and the two seemed to go together. It may be they thought Bob and I were an unappreciative audience, or that we were too small a crowd for them to play to. At any rate, they came no more. I cannot say how Bob felt about it, as he failed to express himself in their absence, but was full of expression during the performance. As for myself, I enjoyed their absence very much indeed.

Trouble on the Trail

We reached the western end of cañon with the sun about one hour high, which was later than our usual time to drive. The grass here, as at the eastern end, was well eaten off by those before us for quite a distance. Our camp hunters, however, had found good grass nearly a mile to the right and around the point of a mountain. So they decided to camp at the cañon's mouth and drive the cattle to the feed, that being nearer than any to be had on the road. Driving them around, all but two of the men returned to camp and ate supper, and a triple guard then went out, three for the fore, and three for the latter, part of the night, as it was always well to be cautious. The wisdom of the course was well proven in this instance.

That evening, as it was getting dark, two men rode up to the camp and, speaking to my brother, said they, with another man, had started from Oregon on horseback to return to the east, with pack animals carrying their outfit. In crossing some river, the name of which I have forgotten, as he told the story, swollen by recent rains, their partner was drowned and their pack horses and provisions lost also. There being a very light emigration on that road, and a poor chance to get anything to eat, they turned across to the California road. The spokesman talked very much as one whose voice was weak from hunger. He said they had had nothing to eat for three days and wanted to buy some food. Brother told him we had nothing to spare in the provision line but, under the circumstances, would have some supper fixed.

But he objected to this, saying they had a camp a mile or two further down and wanted to pay for what they got, as they had not lost their money. Lewis sold them, I think it was, two dollars worth of bacon and beans, some crackers and a little flour. The man handed him a five dollar piece and received his change and they rode away. By some means Lewis failed to put the coin in his purse dropping it into his pocket.

All was a stir at an early hour next morning and those at camp having eaten breakfast, went to gather and drive in the cattle, while the guard came in and ate their breakfast. The order of the day was we would stop at the first good feed and watering place and lie over for the remainder of the day. In the meantime, Lewis putting his hand in his pocket, felt the coin and took it out to put into his purse.

In daylight it proved an easily detected counterfeit. Whereupon he, Mat. and Bob and Abe Dickenson took their pistols, mounted their horses and rode to where the men said they were camped. There, instead of two, they found five men in bed. With arms ready for immediate use, if necessary, Lewis told his man the money received from him was counterfeit and he wanted good

14

money, both for the provisions sold and the change given him. He, of course, expressed great surprise as well as readiness to make good. He said it had been given him in change before leaving the Oregon road. Turning to one of his bedfellows, who kept their positions in bed, he borrowed a twenty-five dollar piece of the same coin, and offered that in making good. Of course, it would have done so for himself, in case he had gotten good money in change again. Upon seeing this, each of our men drew and presented his pistol, and Lewis told them every one to remain motionless while this fellow should immediately pay him in full.

Without further ado, he did so. Our men then rode away, keeping their back eye well open until beyond range of pistol shot.

We drove about five or six miles and, finding feed, etc., camped for the day and night, to give the stock a good rest, as they had been on the go for a week then without it.

That afternoon a man came from the Philips train, then camped at the eastern end of the cañon, asking for help, stating that about twenty head of their cattle had been stolen the night before and they had trailed them well up into the mountains toward the west. Knowing nothing of the number concerned in the theft, they had not a force of their own that was strong enough to risk following them further, and so were seeking help. A couple of trains being in sight ahead and resting as were we, the rider went to them and got two from each. Two of us went with them and three of their own, left up the cañon a short distance to watch, made ten in the company.

We rode up the cañon intending, when opposite the point to which they had followed the trail, to leave the road and reaching that point to follow it until they were overtaken, which those who had followed it that far, thought we would be no great while in doing, as the tracks were quite fresh where they left them.

On coming near the spring at the summit, a smoke was seen rising at the spring. The leader had the rest stop while, leaving his horse, he investigated. In a few minutes he returned saying there were five in number and the cattle there resting, having probably been driven rapidly after getting them away from camp.

15

There being quite a growth of timber and underbrush and those at the spring having a good time, judging from the noise made, we were upon them before they discovered us, every man ready for battle if needful. They were so taken by surprise, and as we discovered, their firearms were with their saddles, they made no effort at resistance.

They were required to saddle their horses, each one under guard while doing so. They were then told to mount, a man holding each horse while they complied, then each had his hands tied behind him and a rope fastened his legs under his horse, and thus mounted all was ready for the start.

They were taken back beyond the eastern end of the cañon to where the train was from which the stock was stolen, and turned over to Mr. Phillips. A guard was placed over them, and a train or two camped further back was notified of their capture.

Next morning there were perhaps fifty men collected from both front and rear trains.

But I forgot to say that, during the night, a posse, or company of four, was sent to the trading post at the entrance to the cañon to arrest two others of their company whose purpose it was to rob the post that night. They were found there, having made arrangements with the keeper to sleep there that night, representing themselves as parties left behind their train looking for some lost cattle. It was no uncommon thing, in case of two or three head escaping the guard, to have some one look through trains following to see if they had fallen in with any of them, as they sometimes did. There was strict honor and honesty among the emigrants that year, at least so far as our observations went. A time or two parties came to our train from before us inquiring if we had lost any of ours, and would go on to the next train or two if not too far ahead, they having picked up some strays.

These men were taken to Phillips' camp and placed under guard with the others.

Next morning a regular court was organized, consisting of judge, jury of twelve and two attorneys, one for prosecuting and one for defending. The case was called, as they were all tried together, it requiring too much time to try them separately. The organizing and trial consumed the entire day until dark, and the Jury were given 'til next morning to bring in their verdict. Of course, they returned to their respective camps to sleep, the judge charging them to discuss the matter with no one and to return in the morning, get together and make up their verdict. They were on hand early and soon had agreed and were ready to return their verdict of "guilty", which was unanimous. During the night one of the attorneys had secured the written confession of one of the two leaders, Lyons and Morgan by name, as given by themselves. They were those who were arrested at the trading post. This confession was written and signed by Morgan in the presence of witnesses and, by permission of the court, was read to the jury before their retiring to make up their verdict.

It was serious, solemn occasion for the judge. There was no question of their guilt, but they could not be turned over to a regular court of law for there was none in possibly hundreds of miles, and there was no way in which they could be secured against further carrying out their avowed purpose of robbing and stealing and possible murder; though up to this time, so far as could be learned, no one had been killed by them, they claimed in their examination that they intended to do their work without killing if they could—but after all to condemn men to death for stealing and robbing only was an extreme penalty. But to turn them loose to prey upon the emigration that was yet to pass along the road was not to be thought of and the court's decision was that the guilty were to be shot.

I say the guilty, for the reason that they all cleared one of two brothers, who were sons of respectable parents and members of a wholesale and retail mercantile firm in one of the leading cities of sacredly secret in every recital of the occurrence made in the state by those present at the time.

The judge's decision was approved, so far as I ever knew, universally by those present, of whom there were more than one hundred at the time of its rendering.

Now, I must relate the fact that perhaps there were none present who were not extremely sorry that there was no other way open to deal with them, except to let them go free, but none that I ever heard of, expressed themselves in favor of that. All this had occupied the better part of another day, and the prisoners were given 'til morning to make any preparation they desired. They disposed of their possessions, consisting principally of their outfit, horses, saddles and arms, each one giving what he had to bestow to those to whom they might have taken a passing fancy.

They all went under fictitious, until in their examination they gave what they said were their true names, except one little fellow whose fictitious name was Badger. He declared, when asked his real name, that he would not give it even if he could have his freedom by so doing. He said his were as respectable and respected parents as any man's, and that he would sooner die than that their name should be disgraced by him. And had it been at all appropriate, he would have been cheered to the echo. As it was, a distinct murmur of approval ran through the crowd.

Somehow or somehow else, by hook or by crook, the two leaders managed to escape during the night.

No one, not even the guards, could give any account of how or when they got away.

The next morning each of the four remaining was given the right to choose by whom he should be shot. There was but one refusal, and that was by a young fellow chosen by Badger, who positively refused. The judge then, as Badger would make no further choice, appointed one whom Badger accepted. He certainly was a brave man and did not seem a bad one, but if not, like poor Tray, was caught in bad company and had to pay the penalty.

They were placed in a line, their eyes bandaged, their hands tied behind them and they were made to kneel down. At a given sign, it was almost as if a single shot had been fired, and as if a single man had fallen, so near together was it that they gave up their lives. Graves had already been prepared, as the people gathered were not conditioned to tarry under the circumstances. As soon as decency permitted, they were buried and the crowd dispersed.

The young man that was unanimously cleared by them as refusing, on all occasions, to take part in their raids on stock or otherwise, was taken in charge by Mr. Phillips and returned to his father, so I heard. He was in the start induced to go from California into the mountains on a professed hunt and, when told what their business really was, wanted to return home, but was informed that, should he make the attempt, he would be killed, under which threat he feared to undertake it.

So ends the most important event, as well as the most solemn, that occurred, as I suppose, on the plains that season.

...The statements of the men agreed quite well with those given in Morgan's confession, so far as I learned what their statements were.

The company was gathered in California entirely, and gave out that they were going to the mountains on a hunting and trapping expedition. Getting well out on the plains, they laid their plans of operation. Having prepared themselves with a counterfeiting outfit, their purpose was, by stealing a few head of cattle or horses from the larger droves, to get enough together to drive to Salt Lake and there dispose of them for material to make counterfeit coin, of which Lewis had for a short time a small specimen.

They had collected one lot and driven there, and disposed of them. They had established headquarters somewhere in the mountains where they kept tools and material stored, while out on their raids and also their stolen stock. At the time of their capture they were gathering their second lot of cattle.

One of their rules, as stated, was never to do any killing, unless it was in fight when on their raids.

It was Lyons and one of the four that was shot that came to our camp with the pitiful story of hunger. It was their purpose, however, to learn how well our camp was protected and what strength of guard was with the stock, as they had, by some means, already learned that the stock were driven some distance away for feed. It so happened that several of the boys were cleaning, oiling and looking after their guns and pistols about the general campfire at the time they came to camp. This, with the number of men present, kept them from an attempt to rob the camp. They had also sent two men to spy out the strength of the guard about the stock.

Seeing so strong a guard, they decided to make no effort to steal any. It was only this timely precaution on the part of our leaders that prevented our having trouble with them. This, however, was only the ordinary custom of the entire trip, and we had never been the wiser of our danger on this occasion had they not told us of it.

BIGNESS

There are a few general things I wish to speak of. There is an enlarged impression of bigness one gets in making that journey, as we made it and others in those days. Bigness of country, of the earth itself, and of things in general. As to impression of one's own largeness, it is much like the Chinaman's promotion in school. He said the professor promoted him backward. One feels as if his enlargedness was increasingly smaller, and that he might be expanded by a great many times his present dimensions without crowding things to any noticeable extent. I think I have seen a great many persons, men of large intelligence in a way, college graduates of high degree, that it would do a whole world of good to make that trip in that way. They manifest a feeling that they fill all the vacant space that can possibly be allowed for one person, and still are badly crowded. Crossing the plains with an ox wagon, and putting in six months of it, would either lead them to conclude there was an abundance of room for several persons of their own mammoth proportions, without disturbing the earth's equilibrium, or crowding any one off it. This impression can be either mental or physical, or both and should prove quite helpful in either or both cases. And if they were not benefited along the line of their particular ailment, it would certainly be because theirs was a hopeless case and they were richly deserving the sympathy of the rest of humanity, inmates of asylums and all.

The greatness of extent, the grandeur of, the apparent everlasting firmness and fixedness, the grand mountains in the distance, pile upon pile, away and away, seemingly limitless, the very mightiness of all. It is inspiring to personal smallness. And yet the invigorating atmosphere, the gentle brilliance of the light inspires to a desire for growth in true greatness; to be a coiner into words, actions and life, of something like the splendor of the scene that lies before one and the feelings that stir your deepest depths.

Many a day, boy that I was, I have driven my team along the road, with an inexpressible desire to flee to the great fountain of all knowledge and wisdom, and learn and learn from and grow, forever and ever; at least, until I could know and be something that was worth being and knowing.

Loretta Burriss Ussery

Homestead
Recipes

Five Generations of Food

Homestead Recipes

Homestead Recipes ~ Five Generations of Food
By Loretta Burriss Ussery

INTRODUCTION

It was happening again. Stepanie and I were sitting in Letty's kitchen with manuscripts spread out on the table when Letty began telling us about Grandma Kate's jersey cow and the thick yellow cream they'd pour over fresh peach cobbler still warm from the oven. Letty had an abundance of stories—both of the foods and the generations of men and women who prepared them. We became convinced that those recipes needed to be collected, as well as the comments and refinements of other cooks who tried, modified, and passed them on. Not only that, there were tales of ancestors and photographs to go with them.

Letty was pleased that we wanted to publish the recipes, but loathe to include stories and photographs. She thought they had no place in a cookbook. I told her there were no rules concerning cookbooks, and since I was the publisher, we could do what we pleased. It seemed such a waste to leave those astonishing stories in our memories when they could be preserved in Letty's own concise and insightful words. At last she agreed. We added a fold-out genealogy in the back of the book, and Letty and Stephanie, who was also an artist, enhanced the pages with charming drawings. We called the book "Homestead Recipes ~ Five Generations of Food."

During California's sesquicentennial, I happened to see a documentary about women in the gold rush. I was surprised. I didn't realize there had ever been any. As a matter of fact, they were rare, but speaker JoAnn Levy asked, "Isn't that what makes something not less valuable, but more?" She had dug into archives, finding the truth expressed in their own words, wrote *They Saw the Elephant: Women in the California Gold Rush,* and corrected the inaccuracy of the historical record by including among the pioneers the most neglected minority in the gold rush era: women.

A number of the vignettes in *Homestead Recipes* are about Letty's gutsy, capable family females who brought with them their own ingenuity, resourcefulness, resilience, wonderful meals, and the ability to make a wild place home.

GRANDMA AND GRANDPA WRIGHT

Grandma and Grandpa Wright rented a place that had been a blacksmith shop. There was a big open fireplace at each end. One end they kept as the living area and one they kept as the cooking area. Grandpa built bunk beds and nailed them to the wall. The floor had cracks in it so Grandpa spread hay all over the floor and Grandma sewed sacks together to make a carpet. They tacked it around the walls so the hay wouldn't come loose. Then she put her braided rugs on it. She loved that place. It shows me that you don't have to have money to make a place homey.

Grandma Wright told me when her mother was having her fourth baby, she was left in charge of the two younger ones. She took them for a ride to keep them out of the house. She put them on a horse and got on behind. When she came back, she leaned over to open the gate to put the horse away, fell off, and broke her arm. She went to her mother, who had delivered the baby, and her mother reached out of the bed, set my grandma's arm, put it in a corset box (which was long and narrow to accommodate the stays), and wrapped it. One must be aware of what a delivery was like at that point in time. That mother had just delivered a baby and then had to set her daughter's arm. No wonder they died early!

The midwife was still there. She thought the arm hadn't been set right, so she unwrapped it and redid it, but she did it wrong and the arm healed a little crooked. Grandma Wright always thought that her arm would have been straight if the midwife had left it alone.

Margaret Ann somehow, as travel was laborious in those days, managed to get to New York from Kansas, where she met a doctor by the name of Hunt and married him there. Later they were divorced and it was considered a scandal. Before this, her sister, Jenny, had gone to Eureka, California. Margaret, in the shame of a divorce, decided to join her sister there, as did their mother, Huldah. Eventually, Margaret remarried. She and Henry Mueller had one son, Clarence.

When the gold rush was in full swing, Henry decided to join the thousands flocking to Alaska. He wrote to Margaret for a while, but then letters came less and less often. She must have felt he was gone much too long and decided to go there herself and appraise the situation. This was a daring thing for a woman to do alone at that time. In the light of what follows, you must realize Margaret was a beautiful woman, exquisitely dressed and groomed, mannerly and proper, with a lovely home, and considered a social leader of her day. Yet she bravely boarded a ship to Alaska, a refined Victorian lady determined to find her husband and bring him home.

When Margaret got to Nome, she surprised Henry and found him living with an Eskimo. It was a terrific shock, but not the worst one. I can see that beautiful, proud, well-dressed woman in the muddy streets of Nome suffering with that knowledge. But she wasn't ready to give up and finally persuaded Henry to come home with her. They boarded the return ship and Henry had his trunk carried to the stateroom. Just before the ship sailed, Henry said he had something he had to attend to, turned around, and left.

When the ship sailed, Margaret realized Henry wasn't aboard. In utter defeat and humiliation, Margaret opened the trunk. It was full of old shoes. He had never meant to go with her. It was a blow from which she never fully recovered.

The Wagon Master

The Wagon Master was my great grandfather. He led four wagon trains across from South Carolina to California. He was 6'4", a giant of a man. He also must have been very dependable. When you signed on with the wagon master, he was boss. He told you where to camp. He decided when to go and where. He had to be trustworthy.

At one of our family reunions, I saw a leather belt he wore. It had a bunch of little pockets and there were notes and money in the pockets. I don't know the purpose of the thing, but he wore it.

On his fourth trip across the United States, Lewis took notes and gave them to his brother, Joseph Newton Borroughs, who was only fourteen when he started West with him. Fifty years later, Joe wrote the story of his trip, which has been published in the book *Journey With The Wagon Master*. At age eighteen Joe became a pastor in Upper Lake, CA, and also taught school. After serving many years in Lake and Sonoma counties, he moved to Oakland. There is a First Baptist Church in Oakland with a stained glass window dedicated in his honor.

Splatter Cake

Splatter Cake—it was named that for its method of assemblage. There is no recipe for this cake. Grandma measured the flour by just putting it in her hand and judging the weight. It was a chocolate cake which nobody knows how to make, but it was a favorite.

My grandfather built a house for Grandma Kate. They lived there a long time. One day, when she was seventy-five, Grandma Kate was walking across the porch and fell through a weak board. She was very upset because she couldn't get out. She hollered and hollered and finally my grandfather came over and took a look. Then he left for a while and came back with a saw and cut her out, but it took a long time. When she was finally free, she marched into the kitchen and made a Splatter Cake. It was then I realized she must have felt completely out of control while waiting there trapped, and what comfort, control, and security there was in the known routine of baking her cake.

Food is orderly. It helps you get yourself back together. Recipes are step by step. It's something familiar in which you are in control. When Grandma Kate fell through the porch, she certainly didn't have any control while she was stuck there waiting for Grandpa. The first thing she did when she got out was cook. I think it was familiar, a comfort, a consolation.

Differing Opinions

Huldah's parents were Eli Bagley, III, and Nancy Ann Belt. This couple and their children were in the Lost Wagon Train coming into Oregon over the Cascade Mountains in the fall of 1853. They were baptized in the Slough of Willamette River. Both of them were buried in California; Eli died in Ferndale, February 22, 1889 and Nancy Ann Belt in Chico, March 20, 1867. On her tombstone are the words "Looking for her three sons in the West." I don't know why, because she knew where they were.

Huldah and David Wright had six children: Emmanuel, James, David Eli, Francis Jenny, Margaret Ann, and Mathias Jonah. Around 1861, David took his oldest son, Emmanuel, who was only fifteen years old, and they both joined the Union Army and went off to fight in the Civil War. During that time they were gone, Huldah stayed alone in the cabin with the other five children. Mathias Jonah was just three.

One early morning, Huldah milked the cow, fed the children, and put the cream on the back of the stove to steep to prepare it for churning. The knock on the thick plank door was a Union Soldier. There were others with him and he asked Huldah if she had food to share with them as they were living off the land as they moved. Then noticing the cream on the stove, he remarked how difficult it must be for her to care for five children by herself and pledged not to steal from them, but only to take what she gave them.

When David and Emmanuel returned, things continued as usual as the town crept to the election year of 1864. The Civil War was still being waged and feeling was still running high. Abraham Lincoln was President of the Union and Jefferson Davis was President of the Confederacy. Old Skinner, David Wright's neighbor, decided to take his team and wagon, asked David to go with him to the nearest polling place. On the way, there was a lot of time for political discussion to get started, and it did. The two men were on completely different sides so the argument grew heated over the merits of Abraham Lincoln and Jefferson Davis. Finally, in loud loyalty, David shouted, "Hurrah for Abraham Lincoln!" Old Skinner said, "Hurray for Jeff Davis!" I can just see him on that wagon being loud—endless miles going to vote. Then he said, "I'm going to kill you for that, Dave." They voted, came home together, Old Skinner let David off at his cabin and drove home. David told Huldah what had happened and so they waited.

As expected, as the two watched out the tiny window of the cabin, they saw Old Skinner returning in his wagon with his rifle. As he reached above the door and lifted his musket off the two brackets, David said, "He's coming to kill me. I'll have to get him first." He opened the door a crack and waited. When Old Skinnner stopped the wagon and climbed down, David aimed and shot him in the leg.

David then loaded him in the wagon and took him home. Upon returning to his cabin, he told Huldah, "I've got to get out of here. Skinner will be back when his leg heals." And so they planned. The place and time for the family to meet was agreed upon and David left on the old gray mare.

As soon as possible, Huldah packed the wagon with their few household possessions, tied the cow on behind, gathered her six children together, and started out to meet David at the appointed place. They traveled for days. On the fifth day, Mathias Jonah, who was driving the team, said, "Ma, I see Dad's old gray mare."

My grandpa, Mathias Jonah, was only six years old at the time, but he remembered all this and told me this story.

Huldah Bagley Wright, my great grandmother, lived to be ninety-three. She still had her own teeth at ninety-three, but everybody told me they were short because they'd just gradually worn down. She always wore a little black velvet bow in her hair.

I love the story of her death. She got up one morning, combed her hair and took her bath out of the bowl, put soda on a rag and washed her teeth (they didn't have toothpaste), brushed that little black bow and put it in her hair, dressed herself, made her bed, laid down on it and passed away.

Son of
South Mountain
& Dust

Thomas W. Wing, D.C., N.D., L.Ac.
and Carolyn Wing Greenlee

Son of South Mountain & Dust

Son of South Mountain & Dust
By Thomas W. Wing
& Carolyn Wing Greenlee

INTRODUCTION

It started with stories about trains. I was a little girl when my dad told me the first one. He had been walking across a wooden trestle fifty feet above the river when a train came rushing toward him. "What do you think I did?" he asked. I had no idea. How could he possibly escape? The bridge was long an he was in the middle. It became my favorite story of his early life.

When I was forty-six, my father was bed-ridden from a cancer surgery that had gone awry. As I stood looking at my usually energetic and talkative father lying limply on his home hospital bed, I tried to remember the details of the train story. How did he escape? I thought I would never forget. And now I couldn't remember. Suddenly I wanted to hear it again. I got a small tape recorder, put it on his chest, and said, "Tell the story about the train, Daddy."

As my dad improved, his restless brain began to run at its normal hyper speed, but he was still confined to bed. What saved his sanity was the tape recorder. Throughout the day and in the middle of the night when he could not sleep he told stories, and every morning I transcribed them. At first the tapes were filled with familiar tales, but soon I was hearing things I had never heard— of a mysterious girl sold at age four during a famine in China to wealthy Chinese San Francisco woman to serve as a maid in her house. The girl was his mother.

Over the months, my father's childhood was spoken before my ears. At last I understood why he would occasionally say the principal had pronounced him the worst kid in the sixth grade. And I knew how he could be a barefoot farm boy in Stockton and the son of a prominent land owner and herb doctor in Modesto at the same time. It was a convoluted history, but the tapes and many questions led to this book, *Son of South Mountain & Dust*. In the process, I understood my father and myself in ways not possible without his stories, this missing piece of history nearly half a century long.

ADVENTURES AT THE RIVER

Past the train station, about a mile down, was the river. There was a lion bridge with two stone lions, one on the end of the hand rails on each side of the walkway that crossed the river. Next to it, on the east side, was a trestle for trains.

I liked to go fishing. There was really nothing else for me to do. My father would not let me work because I was a son of a doctor. My brother would be off some place. We hadn't gone to high school so I didn't really have any buddies. I was a loner at that time. So I would go to the Turner Hardware store, one of the key spots and one of the main emporiums of the farming community. I would purchase a 10¢ roll of fishing line, a float and some hooks and little sinkers. I would go into the back yard and dig up a can of worms. Then I would walk down the railroad track, which was the closest way to get to the river. One of my happiest memories was lying on my back with a piece of grass in my mouth, watching the clouds go by. I guess it was happy because I didn't have any responsibilities or cares or bills. It was a time of carefree childhood freedom.

The actual river wasn't very big, but occasionally it would flood over to the bottom land which was the original river bed eons ago. During Spring's heavy flow, it could crest and flood this area. Mr. Podesto, who owned the property underneath there, had an orchard. The trestle was probably a thousand feet long. The river itself was probably only about twenty feet wide, and very shallow at that time. I'd walk across the trestle timbers, careful not to fall into the river, until I got over to the center part of the river. I would climb down to be off the tracks and sit on the lower horizontal timbers to fish. I'd drop my line down and see what kind of fish I could find.

One time I was going to go fishing by myself, so I started across the train trestle to get to the other side. You put your ear to the track and listen to see if there's a train coming. Well, I decided there wasn't any train coming so I started walking across the bridge. The trestle was a thousand feet long—that's pretty well two or three blocks. By the time I got towards the middle, here comes an unexpected freight train! There was no time to run all the way to the other side, and the drop to the river was maybe fifty feet. That was a long way down. Besides, I couldn't swim. I could have hung over the side, but I didn't want to. What could I do?

On the train trestle they had little water barrels filled with water off to one side. I jumped over into the water barrel and waited until the train went past. I got a little wet, but it was summer, so it didn't really matter. That's the story of how I escaped from getting run over by a train.

CHUN SHEE

My mother was very social and charming, something she learned when she was a maid for a wealthy lady in San Francisco. She was only four years old when her parents sold her to the lady. It was during one of China's many famines. The whole family was starving. My mother told me that her parents told her they loved her very much. They were not selling her so they would have enough money to survive—there wasn't even any food to buy. The only reason they were selling her was she was pretty and young enough that the lady wanted to buy her. She would live in *Gum San* in a beautiful house and learn the gracious ways of the wealthy people she would serve. The family line would live through her in a land

37

full of hope and promise. Her mother wanted her to remember her family name, Chun, so every day she would sit down with her daughter, gather a handful of dirt, and slowly, in front of the little girl, let the dry particles slip through her fingers to the ground. Then she would say, "Always remember, my precious child, our name is Dust."

Can you imagine being four years old, leaving your family and everything you've ever known? There you are, a strange woman holding onto your small hand, taking you to another country where everyone spoke a language you didn't understand. It must have been very frightening for my mother, and very, very sad. She never forgot what her parents told her, and she tried all her life to be kind and generous to other people—especially those less fortunate—and to encourage other people to make the most of their lives.

My mother's early ordeal forced her to become a survivor. The first challenge was surviving the jealousy of the other servants and gaining the favor of her mistress. This gave her the experience and motivation to take advantage of anything she could learn or use. Realizing that, if she didn't learn English she would be confined to Chinatown, she managed to learn to speak without the usual Cantonese accent. Soon she connived to be the undisputed household spokesman and her mistresses's favorite.

This ability to make the most of any situation came in handy when the San Francisco earthquake and fire of 1906 destroyed all birth records. My mother quickly applied for a "duplicate" birth certificate, claiming to have been born in San Francisco. Suddenly she had "proof" that she was an American citizen.

My mother benefitted from being a maid for a wealthy woman. She became social and charming, much sought after for advice on the proper protocol for everything from how to prepare for the birth of a baby to the appropriate arrangements to make for a funeral. It was quite an accomplishment for a slave child.

My mother grew up to be lovely and graceful—a beauty with moon face and almond eyes. She had the creamy ivory skin prized by the Chinese and the gracious ways she had learned in San Francisco. But she never forgot her family name: Dust.

LALU

INTRODUCTION

I hated being Chinese. Then, when I was forty-five, I saw "Thousand Pieces of Gold," a movie about a woman from Northern China sold by her father to serve the men at a silver mine in Idaho. Her Chinese name was Lalu, but the men couldn't pronounce it, so they called her Polly. The movie was fictionalized, but Polly was real.

I was riveted. I had recently learned of my father's mother, also sold to serve, "Whatever that meant," my father said, "Use your imagination."

So I watched. And when I had gazed at the last stunning image of Polly astride a horse, her long black hair loose in the wind, I sat down and this poem poured out. It was the first poem I had written in twenty-five years, and the first ever about being Chinese. It was also the first time I felt proud to be one, and it was because of Polly. At last there was an admirable woman with a face like mine, and it changed me. After that, I eagerly researched the Chinese in Lake County, began giving talks on what it was like to be Chinese in a hostile White world, and of the people of other colors (many of them White) who had been friends with my people including my personal family, and eventually, on the long trip to St. Louis, made a pilgrimage to the little museum in Cottonwood, Idaho, where Polly's belongings and creations are watched over by sweet-faced nuns who come from the convent nearby to open the door for you when you ring the bell.

More than anything I have ever read or seen, Polly's story, made visible by the book by Ruthann Lum McCunn and then the mov-

39

ie, shows me the awakening that becomes possible when something grabs your heart and shakes you out of labels and lies, freeing you to be fully yourself as you were originally created to be. To me, that is the power of story, and of courageous lives, especially when they are true.

LALU

Thick shine
    long sweep
        Chinese hair
            black as ink sticks
            rubbed fine on stone
                watered
            light reflecting whiter
            against the rich dark
Her eyes
    clear
    do not appear
        slanted
        (the embarrassing adjective
                    shaming me)
My soul
    leaps to hers
        grieves her fears
        chafes her captivity
        groans her indignities
        entwines tightly with her
            good brain
      her
        fine heart
Forty-five years
    of other faces
      other hair
        curly
         bright
           blonde
       red
         freckled
          blue
        fluffy
      flashy
  laughing

    curved-calved
        heavy-breasted
        full-hipped
            swaying on stiletto heels

                I—
              clumping in oxfords
           thin sticks terminating in
                Clydesdale hooves
          dark
          plain
          disciplined
          straight-backed Oriental ways
          hard
          as carved teak chairs

Then she
    (who could have been my father's mother)
    drew me as a little child
    called me to live free
        in a wild white place
I embraced her
    kissed her
embraced and kissed myself
braided my hair like hers,
tying the ends in red for happiness

Thick shine
    long sweep
        Chinese hair
            black as ink sticks
            rubbed fine on stone
The wind laughs
        tossing my hair
            black brush strokes
                on wide
                    white
                      sky.

One of the interesting things was that the Chinese were still among the construction crews back in the late '20s. I would walk along the tracks and see cook cars that were either specially made or converted from freight cars. These were the cars in which the Chinese cooks used to prepare food for the crews. The cooks were delighted to see me because they missed their families back home in China terribly. They loved to see a young Chinese child who loved trains coming by.

I didn't speak much Chinese, only a little, but we managed to converse. They would always give me a pie to take home. Apple pie is what they usually made. I didn't get to know them very well, but I do remember that the Chinese crews were on the trains and on the sidings.

There were a lot of single Chinese men back then, not just railway crews. On New Year's, I used to greet them with the traditional saying. *"Gung hay fat choy,"* which means, "May you have fortune." They would smile and give me a $5.00 gold piece. I remember they were very, very lonely.

THE STOCKTON FARM

We lived on Waterloo Road branching off from Cherokee Lane, which was in the south part of Stockton. To get there, you went down the main part of Stockton, turned off on Cherokee Lane, then Waterloo Road, and then passed over this bridge. The farm was on a two hundred acre swath just south of the canal and the levee, which was higher on the Stockton side and lower on our side. When the flood came, the excess water would flow over from this diversion canal to the farm land. Rich soil from the Calavaras River delta would then settle on the farm land and be very good for plowing. We were right there with choice farm land that was automatically fertilized each spring.

Since we were dry farming, we didn't really have to do too much after plowing in the spring after the flood. We'd pull a drill to plant the wheat seeds down, and then just wait. There was no irrigation necessary. It was ideal, especially because we could get premium prices. There was a shortage of wheat after WW1 because people hadn't gotten back to the farms yet. The prices kept rising and rising.

We stayed in the back behind Miss Corey's house in a bunk house made from a converted chicken coop. It was about four feet above the ground because they knew every spring the waters from the Sacramento delta would crest above the river banks and flood three feet. When it did, we'd paddle around on little planks—fun for us. Chickens roosted on the floating planks and ducks quacked as they paddled around.

Miss Corey was the owner of the farm. Apparently her father had been very wealthy and left it to her. Miss Corey was thin and only about five feet tall. She wore a bonnet over her dark hair. Miss Corey never married. She was an old maid. A German fellow worked there. Mr. Miller was a stocky man with a big mustache, broad-brimmed hat, overalls, and iron-clad boots. When I was little (about five or six years old) I was very impressed with the reinforced noses of his big clod boots. He lived in a house in the back and took care of her.

After Kay and I were married, we stopped back to visit him. I took some pictures of Kay sitting in the old carriage with Mr. Miller standing beside her. By then, Miss Corey had died. Probably Mr. Miller was in love with Miss Corey. He never married. Kay thinks they weren't in love. She says they had faithful servants in those days—just faithful people. She says they lived with a love that was a different kind—not the passionate, mad-love kind. I think they never married because of the social differences, but they loved each other all those years. Or maybe he was in love with her. I'm the romantic of the family and I like to think of it like that. Anyway, after Miss Corey was gone, Mr. Miller apparently inherited the farm because he was there when we stopped by to visit, and he showed us around and talked about old times.

My mother was very social and charming. She was always quite a diplomat for doing things properly, so she would visit Miss Corey every so often. Miss Corey didn't have many visitors, even though she was a very nice person. She was very fond of children. My sister Betty was a special favorite of hers. She even took her to church and gave her a Bible.

Miss Corey's house was by the side of Cherokee Lane. In the front of the planed clap board house, there was an arbor near the road with white roses around it. There were trees surrounding the house to keep it cool 'cause it's hot in the San Joaquin Valley. The outside was white with a picket fence all around the house. There was a porch on the front and a big picture window on the left side with beveled-edged glass leaded together in a design. You walked through a large door—oak I think—with a big oval glass insert. It also had beveled edges. Then you'd go into the parlor. Over to the left were a big dark grand piano and a gramophone—an instrument which she wound up, put on the wax cylinder, and you would hear Caruso singing his famous arias. I think this was Edison's first phonograph. Upstairs she had a beautiful built-in tin tub. Then you'd go through to the kitchen.

Miss Corey was an immaculate person. She had a Victorian living room with a beautiful rug and a sofa with needlepoint upholstery. It had cushions stuffed with horsehair that stuck you if you sat on it very long. It'd stick out—you know, the horse hair. On the walls she had beautiful embossed wall paper and pictures made out of dried grass and pressed flowers in a kind of a 3-D effect. People were quite innovative in the old days. I remember the pictures very well. One had a large frame. The picture was about six inches deep. It had flowers and things that were dry in the front and the back was painted in watercolor. I was only six or seven years old, but I had a good memory for those kinds of things. Miss Corey's house was like something you'd see in the movies—a lovely, lovely home. It was like a castle to young people at that time.

One day when my mom was visiting Miss Corey in the living room, I was in the kitchen. She had this beautiful cast iron stove. It was a wood-burning stove because she didn't have gas or electricity. Even though they had those things back then, she didn't have them. The stove had squatty little legs. In the center on the bottom, it had an oven with a white porcelain face on the door. The iron was black and it was immaculately and beautifully kept up. It had these little stove covers on the top. You'd insert a little cast iron handle on a slot on its top and lift them up. In order to make the pot or pan heat faster, you'd open a hole and expose the flame directly to the pots. There were three rings in graduated sizes in each hole—six, eight or twelve inches—different sizes for different sized pots to heat the utensil that was placed over the hole. While my mother was talking to Miss Corey, I was unstacking all the rings and stacking them on the floor. I disassembled the stove. My mother was so embarrassed she never took me to Miss Corey's house again.

AT THE PEA PLOT

As soon as the sun rose, the farm hands were off to work. I showed up in my roadster a few hours later (after all, I was the owner's son). At the bunkhouse/kitchen/eating area, I asked what I could do. You could see the wheels going around in How Say Gor's head as he rubbed his whiskered, unshaven chin. He was trying to think of the easiest and least uncomfortable job to assign me. I was probably considered more of a nuisance than a help, although they all enjoyed a youngster who was interested enough to volunteer. "Why don't you take this gourd of tea and crackers to Chern Goh, who is at the peas and see if he can use your help." (Chern was his given name. Goh is always added meaning something like "brother.")

As I approached the pea plot, I admired the uniformity of the neat rows, row after row of peas. Each group of pea vines was supported by four bamboo poles that met to form a tepee-like tent which allowed the maximum exposure to sun and ease of picking the pods. The workers lovingly trained the leader vine to entwine around each pole and grow to the top.

As I paused under one of the trees to rest in the shade, I saw Chern Gor in the distance heading down to the irrigation ditch. Across his shoulders was a pole about five feet long. On each end hung a kerosene tin that had been made into a watering can. The tops were cut off, carcinogenic petroleum traces cleared with the juice of lemons or pineapple. A large metal spout was soldered at the bottom with its sprinkler head reaching above the top rim. This made it possible for Chern Gor to carry the water without spilling it. Two wires made the handles.

Chern Gor dipped one of the cans into the water of the irrigation ditch and, in one quick swoop, filled it to the brim. In the same motion, he filled the empty can on the other end of the pole. I was amazed that he could fill both cans practically without stopping. He performed this like a ballet dancer, a symphony of motion and precision. In a few seconds, he was back on his way to the pea patch. Carefully balancing the load across his broad shoulders, he trotted down the narrow path between the planting towards the growing pea plants. Trotting? I became interested. Water weighs eight pounds per gallon. Each can held five gallons. Two cans weigh eighty pounds. The yoke pole weighted about another ten pounds. I noticed he trotted in rhythm. At each bounce of the pole, he timed himself so that the weight of the load would lessen, so part of the time his load was less than pure dead weight. He was using the science of action/reaction and the spring rate of the pole to make the ninety pounds seem to be, say, only half the weight on each bounce up. I wondered—how could an uneducated person know this? You can see how astounded I was to realize the amount of science he was using. Even as a teen, I was seeing things from a scientific viewpoint instead of just seeing a laborer carrying water—and my opinion of the Chinese peasant was instantly transformed.

At each individual plant, Chern Gor tilted one can to pour out a measured amount of water into a small basin at the base of each plant. As the amount of water delivered began to unbalance the watering cans, Cher Gor deftly shifted to pour from the other. I knew right away that I could never do this, and the admiration of these humble workers has never left me.

As I waited for Chern Gor to finish his watering, I found relief from the boiling sun by sitting inside the pea leaf tepee. It was the only source of coolness in the scorching valley heat. As soon as Chern saw me, a big smile crossed his weathered face. *"Hola mah? (How are you?)"* he said in *Sam Yup,* our Cantonese dialect. Then he courteously squatted down beside the teepee to fish out a Chinese rice bowl from the picnic basket I had set down inside another tepee. He put some saltine crackers into the bowl and carefully spooned on some white sugar. Then he removed the cork stopper from the gourd. The cork had a string nailed to its top. Chun Gor let it dangle from its string which was tied to the small of the neck of the gourd. He carefully poured the cool tea over the crackers and offered me the first serving to eat with a Chinese porcelain spoon. But first he told me to wait until the crackers had softened.

I sat on the ground, but the Chinese never do. They squat. This is a lot more scientific since they sit on their haunches for hours without getting tired. As I spent time observing them at work, I realized that through the millenniums past, the methods developed by Chinese workers were honed and passed down for the benefit of their people.

Chern Gor took the opportunity after his tea break to roll a cigarette from the bag of Bull Durham and refill papers he always carried in his hip pocket. He licked the edges of the roll to paste them together, struck a match on the bottom of his shoe, and took a puff. "Little brother," he said, "Don't start smoking like I do. It's a bad habit. Also don't drink or gamble either. These are bad things, so don't start in." I didn't know much Sam Yup Cantonese except what I picked up talking to my father, but I listened and tried to understand. I asked him about his family in China. He said he wished he could send more money or go home himself, but he had only recently been able to pay off his passage and must stay longer to show a profit. He said if he knew life would be so difficult in *Gum San,* he would never have come here. The word he used meant more than hard work. It meant terribly hard. Many difficulties.

Almost every single one of them had the same lament. I felt sorry for them. It was such hard, backbreaking work. Also, in China, you could only work so many hours—sun up to sun down. As soon as it's night, you quit. But here, there were electric lights and you continued to work. During the day, they'd tend the crops, pick the beets, for example. Then, during the night, they carried the beets into the shed, washed and tied them up. They worked such long hours. In China, after dark you'd be home. You'd have your wife to feed you, rub your back, and feel sorry for you. Here, there was nothing to comfort them from their bitter difficulties.

THE WOES OF CHINESE MEDICINE

The first record of a Traditional Chinese Medicine practitioner in California was Yee Fung Cheung who came from my father's homeland, Guangdong Province, to make his fortune during the gold rush in 1850. He found mining the sick for gold was better than washing dirt in cold water and soon had a growing practice among his own race. Later, as his fame for curing the sick spread and due to the shortage of any doctors of any kind, he had Caucasian patients as well as Chinese.

Ironically during the peak of the anti-Chinese period, Leland Stanford, who was inaugurated as Governor on his "banish the Chinese-stand," found his wife near death. His Chinese cook asked Cheung to treat Mrs. Stanford. He cured her. This helped diffuse the anti-Chinese hysteria, and other Chinese herbalists such as Ing Hay and Wing Luke of Seattle made the transition to treat Caucasians as well as the Chinese community. Anti-Chinese hysteria had practically vanished when my father arrived thirty years later. He inherited Dr. Yee's pioneering legacy in Chinese herbs, which were now being widely accepted by Caucasians. He was readily accepted as a respected physician in the White community.

These early pioneers had racial prejudice to deal with, but they did not have to face the medical persecution that occurred when Fishbein, Secretary of the AMA, decided to have MDs monopolize medicine. Using lobbying and politics, he tried to eliminate every other medical practitioner, including chiropractors, osteopaths and Chinese herb doctors. That's when my father's troubles began.

One of my first memories was of my father's knees. I was grabbing his legs when the policeman arrested him to take him to jail for practicing medicine. I think it was around 1920. As I can recall, he'd be arrested in the morning, go to jail, and come out that afternoon. Then he'd go to the grocery store and buy oranges and things to bring home to the family.

As my brother and I grew older, my father would have us deliver Christmas presents to the judge and the civic people. We didn't realize at that time what was happening, but later on, we resented it. We said, "Why should we be giving them things when they arrested him all the time?" Later on, I realized what it meant.

The judge's name was Fulkert. In Modesto, they named a road after him. Even in Merced there was a Fulkert Road. He was the one, when my father was arrested, that they came before. Judge Fulkert would say, "Guilty or not guilty?" They'd say, "Guilty." And he'd say, "Fine, so much." As we grew older, he had us take Christmas presents to the judge. And we said, "Why does he do that when the judge always fines him?" Then we learned if you plead guilty and are fined, they arrest you over and over and over again. It doesn't make any difference. But if you appeal it and you're found guilty, then it becomes a felony. The judge always just fined him a very small sum of money. So giving the presents to the judge did do some good, but we didn't know that.

FCF

In 1910 and 1911, before World War I, my father invented an herb formula which he called "FCF" for "Flu-Colds-and-Fever," which he dispensed the usual Chinese way—going to his herb room and wrapping in individual paper packets a week's supply of herbs (which were different combinations of medicinal roots, bark, twigs, seeds, etc.).

Each day the patient would boil one packet's worth of herbs for an hour, strain out the residue, and then drink the brew. To make it more palatable, my father would include a prune as a sweet desert.

Chinese herbs are not specific like vaccines or antibiotics. Their theory is to prescribe the herbs that will balance and strengthen the body which has become unbalanced from the illness. In this way herbs help return the patient to health no matter whatever the disease or how the bacteria or virus mutates. That's why FCF was so effective in the Great Flu Epidemics of 1911, 12, and 14. So after the Flu Epidemics, my father had a tremendous practice. He had been doing well as a practitioner before, but he reached his zenith in the Flu Epidemic of 1914. He had quite a reputation. That's how he made his fortune.

From 1917-1919, we had another flu epidemic. It took everybody down the line. My father was very smart during that time. He had his people go around house to house and distribute the herbs free with "N.S. Sue Herb Company" written on the packets. By then, so many needed the formula that he couldn't distribute it as a regular bunch of herbs you had to boil. What did he do? He ground up the herbs with a corn grinder like they use on the farm—a couple of coarse blades with teeth on it that rub together. He dropped the raw herbs in and this little circular feeder fed the herbs in and ground them up. With the powdered herbs, it was only necessary to add a cup of hot water, stir and drink the tea.

It also no longer looked like branches, leaves, and roots and berries, so even the Caucasians found it acceptable. My father gave FCF to everyone in Modesto and many got bet- ter faster. After the epidemic, they did not forget him. Most Chinese physicians had only Oriental patients, so they stayed in Chinatown. In my father's case, he had only Caucasian patients—the Fire Chief, the Chief of Police—all of the important people of the town. So we grew up comfortably in the company of other races.

I remember when I was very small, I'd take a little wagon and go down the street and pass out samples of N.S. Sue's herbs for u. My father had advertising printed on the little envelopes in which he packaged his herbs. On his packages of FCF, he claimed to have saved thousands during the u epidemics of 1911-14, and 1917-19.

FINDING SOMETHING TO HAUL

When I was in my teens, my father bought a farm with a Japanese partner. My brother and I were old enough by then to drive trucks delivering our produce to the markets. Since we only serviced the markets one or more times a week (depending on the season), after we had replenished the warehouse the truck was idle. During the summer there was opportunity to haul fruit—usually peaches—as Modesto also had Tri-Valley Cannery.

Because I had no Chinese accent, when I'd call on the telephone and say, "Mr. Brown, do you have peaches you want hauled?" He'd say, "Yes, I do have that job. How much a ton are you asking?" The ordinary thing was $2.00 a ton to pick it up in the orchard and haul it to the market. I'd say, "I'll haul it for a dollar and a half a ton. He says, "Fine. When can you come to work?"

Well, when I'd show up for work, he'd see some little seventeen-year-old Oriental kid. He'd say, "Who's the boss?" and I'd say, "I am."

"You're Chinese?"

"Yes."

"Oh, I'm so sorry. My partner just gave the job to somebody else. He didn't know that I had talked to you about it."

Everywhere, it was the same. No matter what I charged, they wouldn't give me the job. But I knew there was one thing they didn't mind if we hauled, if we were doing it for ourselves.

We found we could buy manure and resell it to farmers. The usual price was $1 a ton, and you received $2 a ton delivered to the farm.

Before we approached the manure farm, we weighed the empty truck. We then loaded up about five tons of manure, went to the weigh scale where we paid about 25¢ to have the truck weighed, and then we paid the farmer for the load. Each time we would load the manure, we stopped when the rear license plate was six inches from the ground. Each time, the load came to five tons.

We asked the farmer if we could eliminate the time spent weighing and coming back to pay for the manure since the load was always five tons when the rear license plate was six inches from the ground. At a dollar a ton, the load would cost us $5. The farmer said that would be okay if we paid him $6 for the load. The farmer knew the one and a half-ton Chevy couldn't carry any more than five tons. So then he made a dollar more than if we had weighed it.

What the farmer didn't know was that the Super Truck could carry more than five tons. By loading the manure higher in front instead of evenly across, the weight was shifted toward the front and much more load could be carried before the license plate reached six inches from the ground.

Once we made one load so heavy that the truck wouldn't run except in low gear, so we had it checked, the truck weighed 28,000 pounds—or nearly twelve tons! The scale man couldn't believe the scale and rechecked and rechecked, but it was still 28,000 pounds! We knew the truck weighed 4,400 pounds. All the rest was manure. We paid $6 for that load, and sold it for $24—a profit of $18 instead of $5.

I tell you, pitching manure on and off of a truck with a shovel isn't what you would call gravy train work, but I had the satisfaction of knowing that my specially-designed suspension and tires and my scientific method of loading more than doubled our profit. It was one of the things I did using technology to offset prejudice. Still, I didn't feel right about that deception even though the farmer thought he was cheating us. Two wrongs don't make a right, so I told my brother we would quit hauling manure.

Note from Carolyn: My dad loved trucks, trains, planes, cars, and all things mechanical. His dream was to become a truck driver, but his father had other plans. He wanted him to be an herb doctor like him. My father resisted. At length, his father made him an offer—you go to school for two years to be a doctor and, if you don't like it, you can quit and be a truck driver., My father happily agreed. After two years of college, he told his father he didn't like it and still wanted to follow his dream, so his father acquiesced.

My dad spent some hard months trying to make a living in his chosen field, but after being on the disheartening end of racial prejudice, he went to Los Angeles Chiropractic College, became a doctor of chiropractic, and opened his practice as a DC, but his real success was in Chinese herbs. People flew in from all over the world to get his treatments because he was curing Type 2 diabetes with herbs in two months.

In 1973, my father's love of electronics and his expertise in Chinese medicine came together in his invention of medical microcurrent. It revolutionized electronic medicine, especially in sports medicine where it went to several Olympics, but that's another story in another book. As I see it, if it hadn't been for that racial prejudice, my father might have spent his life innovating and improving vehicle function, but the world would have missed the combination of his most brilliant inventions in the coalescing of his greatest and most creative gifts.

A
SAGA
of
SCOTTS VALLEY

Loretta Burriss Ussery

A Saga of Scotts Valley

A Saga of Scotts Valley
By Loretta Burriss Ussery

INTRODUCTION

The first book Curator Donna Howard asked us to bring back into print was *A Saga of Scotts Valley* by Loretta Burriss Ussery. My assistant Stephanie and I were soon friends with the energetic elderly woman. Together we decided to give her book a new look, added photos and a fresh layout. For the cover, Stephanie used a section of one of Letty's oil paintings—the house her great grandfather built. That house was especially dear to us because it was in its tidy kitchen that we heard so many wonderful stories and brought two more books into print.

A Saga of Scotts Valley is more than the history of a place and the people who lived there. It's bits of memories shared by individuals who lived in the original homesteading era. Letty did the diligent collecting, the writing, the remembering, in the hope that people will realize they're involved in history. What seems insignificant today becomes treasured memories later.

Letty believed everyone is part of their own history, and everyone is part of the history of the world. Because of that, she said we need to pay attention to our own lives and roots, and to others. We need to appreciate that it's all part of who we are. "Write it down," she said. "Don't lose it. It's too valuable to forget."

THE GAME WARDEN AND THE TWO BOYS
DON LEE PATTEN

A few days before quail season opened, Don Lee Patten and Stanley Gavette were tramping around Scotts Valley trying out Stanley's new gun.

Late in the afternoon when the two young boys were growing tired, Harve Meador pulled up beside them in his old Whippet car and asked if they wanted a ride. They accepted, climbed into the back seat and rode slowly down the road with Harve.

In the meantime, someone had called the Game Warden and reported two boys shooting in the Valley. Jack Sawyer answered the call and when he spotted the two boys in the car he pulled across the road in front of the old car with a grand flourish, apparently to keep the Whippet from making a fast get-a-way.

When he approached the car he told them of the report and began to search the car. When he reached under the seat and pulled out a burlap sack with the contents still warm, he said with great satisfaction, "I've caught you this time."

He opened the sack, reached in for the evidence and pulled out the dead cats Harve was taking to the dumps to bury.

No one remembers Jack Sawyers remarks, but the two boys do remember the grin on Harve's face as he sat placidly chewing tobacco.

The Determined Buck Hunters
Ross Voreis

My story is about three young boys who were trying to become buck hunters in the early days.

It wasn't easy getting invited along on those hunting parties. Our fathers were working seven days a week and when the men did decide to get away they didn't want "no snot nose kids" messing them up. We would hear all the stories, year after year, when the men got back with all those beautiful bucks. Every year we would dream and plan about the time when we would get to go. We had been on every trail, knew every spring and where the camps were because we lived in the hills whenever our folks would permit it. By this time we could hit a rabbit on the run and track animals for miles. Our hat bands were full of rattlesnake rattles until one of our folks read where someone went blind doing that, so from then on, it was coon tails instead of rattles.

The three young boys in this story are Archie Hendricks, Jr., Bill Wambold and myself, Ross Voreis.

This particular year we decided it was time to put a little pressure on if we were to ever get invited so Bill's mother, who was the only daughter of George Pool, was our ally and through her efforts we were on our way.

There were three main campsites on the Scotts Valley watershed and far enough apart that none interfered with the other. There was Hendricks camp, Pool camp and Lindeblad camp. The trails to each camp were maintained and each camp did its share of control burning providing an abundance of feed and deer. George Pool was ramrod of the Pool camp and had a string of mules he used to pack in supplies before the season opened.

The big day arrived and I'm sure if the other boys were like me they couldn't sleep for being keyed up. We were told to go to the Pool camp a day ahead of the men as none of us had horses and it was a long walk. I'm sure they thought we would go back home before any of them arrived, but they didn't know us very well.

We made crude packs out of gunny sacks that we put out old World War I blankets in along with other things we thought were precious and useful for our survival kits, but which to this day would make a sane person shudder.

We left early on a Thursday morning and I couldn't tell if our mothers were apprehensive or not. The trail we took started in back of the Archie Hendricks place and took us to the top of Little Cow Mountain where we followed the ridge to Hendricks Opening. There we branched off down into Hendricks Creek then up through Stoney Opening. The deer, quail and rabbits were everywhere and we spotted four nice bucks along the way. Mr. Cunningham, of Ukiah, ran thousands of sheep in the Cow Mountain Range in those days, but always moved them out before deer season opened. Any that were left behind belonged to anyone who wanted them.

As we were going through Stoney Gap Opening there were four stray sheep looking very lost. Since George Pool told us to provide some camp meat for him we drove the lost sheep down the trail into camp thinking they would be great for camp meat and we wouldn't have to waste a shell. None of us owned anything but a .22 rifle so for this big event we borrowed 30-30 rifles and I mean we could have taken on the whole German army feeling as we did with those rifles in our hands. We had one box of shells between us and we had pooled our resources to get that. Our feelings were with 20 shells we could get 20 bucks. That's how confident we were. We made it into camp with our meat supply and they were ready to rest so we didn't have to tie them up.

Off we went to the beautiful spring to get a good drink of water taking turns lying on our stomachs to drink our fill. Bill was last when I was conscious of him slipping backwards or crawling backwards. We had lots of early training pretending to crawl up on bands of wild Indians without being detected, but this was a new technique. When I asked, "What's the matter, Bill?", he was white so I looked where his eyes were concentrated and there was a big rattlesnake all coiled up just above the water. It was a close call but we had one more set of rattles.

The day was getting short so we cooked up some food from our meager supply, ate and then had a good shower from the spring. That night was uneventful except we were all thinking of the big hunt on Saturday.

The next morning we had a quick breakfast and had to track the sheep down again and bring them back to camp. This time we tied them up with some rope George had left from his previous supply trip. That done, we hiked back down the trail part way to meet George who always came in early to set up camp. We could see George really didn't need our help with the mules so we went exploring the best place to hunt the next day.

It wasn't long before we heard and awful bellow from camp so we trotted back to find George very unhappy with those sheep eating up all the good graze from his mules. He soon put us to work butchering two of the youngest and then driving the other two back to Stoney. That day George cooked up one of the biggest mutton stews you ever saw and of course, there were three hungry boys to help eat it and to this day I've never eaten anything better.

That evening with a full moon and a big bonfire, the hunters started to arrive on horseback and every dog thought it was his very own camp and would fight to prove it. By 10 O'clock things were a bit hairy around there and I for one wished I was someplace else because we couldn't seem to keep out of the way. By 11 O'clock the last dog was tied and the last horse unsaddled and the social aspect of deer hunting came into focus. As the bottles were passed around the buck hunting got into full swing and during that whole evening there wasn't a buck that got away. To this day it's a mystery to me how they've managed to propagate themselves. We couldn't contribute anything to the stories that night around the campfire, but someday we knew we would.

The next morning was bedlam while getting breakfast, feeding the dogs, saddling the horses and checking the guns. Finally everything was in readiness when someone said, "What the hell are we going to do with these kids?" Well, there were no rocks to get under so we just stood there with our guns at the ready as he sounded like he wanted to do away with us. George, thank God, said, "Go on, I'll take them with me." He took us to a little ridge overlooking a large area not far from camp and told us to keep a sharp lookout. We settled down, each facing a different direction, and with the break of day it sounded like the war was on. Deer were running every which way, but to our disappointment there were no bucks that came our way. From all that shooting and hollering we asked George if they were getting our bucks too, but he didn't seem to think so. From all the bucks killed around the campfire the night before I could just see bucks lying dead everywhere.

About three in the afternoon it got awfully hot on that Ridge and George said he would go back to camp and cook dinner. A dog every now and then would chase a deer and bark so we still had hopes. The rest of that day we spent clearing the brush off that ridge so we could see better and I mean we worked. We finally ran out of water, it was getting dark and we were getting hungry so we returned to camp. We were disappointed to see no hunter had brought a buck in yet, but soon one arrived, then another, but that was only two and there were at least 40 shots fired that day.

That night around the campfire we were anticipating another big kill. The bottles were passed around, but the buck stories didn't. There were mostly stories about women and what did we care about that?

The next morning things were better organized and the hunters went out with more determination. We three went back to our Ridge and George stayed in camp. With all our work on the Ridge, we could now see better and had a good clear field of fire in any direction. As day broke again the shots were more spaced and you could tell they were doing better.

About noon some wise old dog got on this buck's track and jumped him in our direction. You could just tell he was going to knock us off our Ridge so we lined up there abreast. When he came flying up that Ridge at us it was as if someone told us when to fire because we all let go a shot at the same time and the old buck dropped not 25 feet from us. George heard us yell and came up to see what we had. I'm sure there have been bigger bucks killed, but to us it was the biggest ever. It seemed even larger coming up that hill at us. There was only one bullet hole in the neck, but all three of us killed that buck.

Now there is one more story for the telling around the campfire and George thereafter always referred to our Ridge as Baldy - a tribute to three determined kids.

The Life and Death
of a Quicksilver Mine

by Helen Rocca Goss

The Life and Death of a Quicksilver Mine

The Life and Death of a Quicksilver Mine
By Helen Rocca Goss

INTRODUCTION

When I was collecting information for my book *Once There Were Thousands,* I read everything I could find on the Chinese in Lake and surrounding counties, from historian Henry Mauldin's collected eye-witness statements and stories, to every article that appeared in newspapers of the area from 1874, the year my great grandfather Gong arrived in San Francisco, to 1920 or so, when the anti-Chinese hatred had finally died down. It was grueling and sad and sometimes downright horrifying. I wondered if that was how everyone saw my people. Were we really believed to be that despicable, that worthless, that unregenerate, our value considered to be less than a dog's?

But then Curator Donna Howard suggested I read *The Life and Death of a Quicksilver Mine.* I had no idea I would encounter the clear-eyed insight of a Victorian woman named Helen Rocca Goss, or that I would find a hero in her father, Andrew Rocca, Superintendent of the Great Western Mine.

What I read astonished me. Helen Goss wrote that her father demonstrated not only concern for the well-being of his workers, he even learned to speak Cantonese. Friendships developed, respect and affection grew between workers and the Rocca family members.

Even though she was only a child at the time, young Helen knew quite a few of the workers by name, vividly recalling in later years their habits, characteristics, and character. In her stories there are no hordes, teeming and threatening masses of filthy, immoral, indecent Celestials. She wrote of individuals, many of whom she remembered with fondness.

I deeply desired to include portions of Helen Goss' book in *Thousands,* but there was no way to get permission. Her book had gone out of print, she had gone to Heaven, and I could not locate her heirs, so I gave up. I was not going to publish my book without her words to balance the appalling newspaper articles I had originally planned to include in my book.

Two decades later, Donna Howard happened to attend one of my talks. Afterwards I told her I had given up on my book and when I explained why, she said a letter had come to the museum requesting information on someone named Rocca. It was several years ago, but I might still be able to reach him. Not long after, she sent me his address.

Bart Rocca responded swiftly and took the matter to the family for consideration. They gave their permission. Then Roy Rocca sent photographs from the book. I was ecstatic. Though I ended up deciding not to publish *Thousands,* I realized many of my favorite stories of the Rocca family fit into my new book perfectly. Once more, I contacted Bart and Roy, and once more they gave me permission on behalf of their family.

As I began writing the introduction to this section, it occurred to me that I knew very little about Andrew Rocca or the relationship Bart and Roy had with him, so I sent them another email. Roy emailed the following:

"Andrew Rocca is our great grandfather, our father's father's father. He left his native town of Borgonovo, Italy, in Oct. 1853 and arrived in New York that December. He then traveled on via the isthmus of Panama to San Francisco, arriving in January 1854."

With a start, I realized Andrew Rocca was a First Generation Italian immigrant. That means he arrived fluent in Italian, but not necessarily in English, which makes his learning Cantonese even more impressive. It is a very difficult language.

To my knowledge, there is not another book like *The Life and Death of a Quicksilver Mine* written with kindness by an eye witness of that tumultuous time. It is my honor to bring these stories back into print, and to help preserve this extraordinary legacy created by an exceptional man from a far away place, a legacy that continues graciously flowing through the Rocca family to this day.

THE GREAT WESTERN MINE

In the autumn of 1876, my father, Andrew Rocca, became superintendent of the Great Western Quicksilver Mine, a post he continued to hold until May, 1900. The mine, which was one of the most important in California throughout those twenty-four years, was in Lake County.

Almost all of the labor at the mine was Chinese, the number of them usually varying from two hundred to two hundred and fifty. Only the foreman, the office employees, the storekeeper, the teamsters, the engineers--about twenty-five men in all--were White. The Chinese lived in two camps, the earlier and larger one always called the No. 1 Camp, the second sometimes referred to as the No. 2 Camp, but, for a reason which no one remembers, more often designated "The Brown China Camp." The men came from different parts of China, and, of course, spoke various dialects, but those in the No. 1 Camp were mostly from the Canton area. There were two distinct types of Chinese at the mine--the coolies, who spoke little or no English and lived very primitively in the "China camps," and the superior, educated men who managed their business affairs for them, held the more important underground jobs, worked in the store, or in the superintendent's home....

There was no central eating place in either camp, and each man made his own small fire to cook his rice and heat the water for his tea. If one chanced to pass either camp at meal time, he could look through the open doorways and see the squatting men eating their bowls of rice with chopsticks. The men generally wore what a member of the family describes as "a kind of dungaree costume similar to the work clothes of sailors," plus the characteristic large woven straw hat which identified them even at a distance.

LEADERS

Each camp had a leader or boss who kept time for all of his own men and acted as their business representative on all occasions, especially on pay day. At that time the boss would come to our home to work out with Father the amount to which each man under the boss' jurisdiction was entitled. The entire sum was paid to the boss, and he was then responsible for paying the individual work-men in his camp. The necessary calculations arriving at these sums were made on the abacus, an aspect of pay day which was a source of fascination for the children in our family. If we remained very quiet, we were permitted to watch this mysterious and enchanting process.

The camp bosses also served as mediators in disputes among their men, disputes which were by no means infrequent. Next to the men who presided over the Chinese section of the mine store, the bosses were the best educated of the Chinese. One of them in particular, Ah Shee, who served as boss of the Brown China Camp for many years, was a very capable and outstanding man, a great friend of my father's and, indeed, of all the family. Ah Shee was not only his camp boss, but he was head timberman as well, and many of the enormous timbers used in the mine--some as much as three feet in diameter--were so well placed under his direction that they still stand in a section of the Great Western where they have been preserved by the mineral water dripping over them. Ah Shee was larger than most of the other Chinese at the mine, a fairly well-educated man, and one of the best workmen as far as character and trustworthiness are concerned. His wage of $1.50 a day was the highest paid to any Chinese working underground. Only Ah Tie, who was paid $1.75 for about fifteen hours of duty in the store, earned more.

Ah Shee entrusted his savings to his employer, who kept a special account for him at the Bank of California in San Francisco. By the time he was ready to return to China, Shee had saved nearly $6,000. Once he came to the house to withdraw $100, explaining that the sum would be sent to his son in China for the purpose of buying a wife. It would, he added, buy "a heap fine" wife. After we left the Great Western in 1900 and moved to the Helen Mine about ten miles away, Ah Shee kept up his friendship with his old employer by walking across the hills to visit us as often as he could.

He never arrived empty-handed, always bringing some choice Chinese gift, such as a package of the finest China tea for Father, or an exquisite silk handkerchief for Mother. Ah Shee's gentleness, his unfailing courtesy, and his strength of character won him the respect and friendship of all mine inhabitants, Chinese and White alike, and he was a special favorite of the children.

It was Ah Shee and Ah Key, for a long time the boss of the No. 1 Camp at the Great Western, who used to bring us the long strings of firecrackers, the bounteous supplies of candy, nuts, and the like at Chinese New Year. Ah Key was a small, neat man with a less interesting personality than Ah Shee, under whom he served as first assistant in timbering. Key was a very valuable man, though, in helping to keep the peace among the various factions, not only in his own camp but in the other camp on occasion. Once there was a bad flare-up of tempers in Ah Shee's camp, and the superintendent hurried over there as soon as he learned of the trouble. When he returned home he remarked that by the time he arrived Ah Key was there and had restored order adding: "You can always depend on Ah Key."

THE CHINESE MUST GO

Andrew Rocca's ability to converse with the men in their own language naturally endeared him to them, and he in turn had a real affection for them. That the relationship between employer and employees was not unlike that between a parent and small children was particularly evident in one phase of "The-Chinese-Must-Go" campaign in California. The State Legislature had begun passing discriminatory legislation aimed at the Chinese as early as the middle of the '50s, and the Constitution adopted by California in 1879 invited even more stringent laws of this kind by requiring the legislature to set up the conditions under which objectionable persons might reside in the state. One of the laws passed under this provision prohibited corporations holding state charters from employing "any Chinese or Mongolian" and established heavy penalties for violation of the law.

The legislation had an immediate and paralyzing effect on the quicksilver mines, which depended almost wholly on the Chinese for their underground labor. In a letter of February 14, 1880, Andrew Rocca wrote his fiancee: May, it made my heart ache…when I had to discharge all my Chinamen right in a snow storm, to… but I had to do it." He added that he believed "the poor creatures would sooner go to their death than be discharged."

The president of the nearby Sulphur Bank Mine deliberately defied the law so that he would be arrested and tried. In the test case against him, the Circuit Court, on March 22, 1880, handed down a strong opinion, which held the law in contravention of both the Burlingame Treaty and the Fourteenth Amendment to the Constitution. Two days later Andrew Rocca reports in another letter to his fiancee the good news that about one hundred and fifty of "his Chinamen" were already back at the mine and that he would add another hundred Chinese as soon as possible.

GAMBLING

While it is clear that women did not figure greatly in the existence of these hard-working Chinese, whose hopes and desires centered around a return to their native land, the gambling vice, which often postponed the realization of that home-going dream, did play considerable part in their lives. All of the older members of the family remember what they compositely describe as "the sleek, dainty-handed, city-looking, foppish, Chinese gamblers," who came regularly after pay day to gather in the spoils; how the monotonous sing-song of a fan-tan game would go on for hours; how Father's temper and blood pressure would mount as he heard those unmistakable sounds of the presence in camp of the traveling professional gamblers, whom he so thoroughly detested. When he could stand it no longer, he would set out for the China camps, armed with his cane.

70

The entry in my mother's diary for May 24, 1891, reads in part: "Mr. R. raided Chinese gamblers last night. ($115)." To this terse statement members of the family are able to add some interesting details of what the raids were like. My older brother, for example, writes of going with his father through the No. 1 Camp when gambling was in progress. A pile of dried beans was placed on a table and then the men would bet with the professional gambler on whether the number of beans was odd or even. With a chopstick, the gambling man would then slide two beans at a time off the table, while the other Chinese sat very still and watched intently. As he neared the end of the pile, the man would use a long fingernail, or his little finger just under the chopstick, to remove an extra bean, if he saw that necessary in order to win the bet. "Young as I was," my brother writes, "I could see what was going on, but the Chinese workmen apparently didn't. After watching a few moments, dad took his cane, scattered money and beans all over the place, then clubbed the offenders over the head."

CHINESE NEW YEAR

The Joss House, which stood on a hill above and a short distance from the larger Chinese camp, served as both social hall and chapel for the Chinese. It was a square, barn-like building with large pictures on the walls of various Chinese rulers and deities, as well as of the devil, in front of which punks were kept burning. The religion of the men seemed to be based more on fear of the devil than on worship of any one god.

It was on a flat in front of the Joss House that the biggest event of the Chinese year was held--the festivities associated with their New Year, falling on a date sometime between late January and the third week in February. The White families at the mine had so large a share in this festival that they came to think of it as one of their own holidays. Each year my mother made mention of the celebration in her diary, and in one of the letters to her family in her early married life, she wrote,

The Chinamen celebrated their New Years about a week ago. We were well remembered, receiving from different ones about a doz. silk handkerchiefs, a doz. live chickens and a big turkey, with any quantity of oranges, candy, nuts, preserved fruits, American cakes and Old Burbon & Cigars. They are very generous at such times.

As the above quotation suggests, the superintendent's family was overwhelmed with presents at the time of the Chinese New Year celebration, and, in fact, the gifts began arriving long before the actual festival. The first thing to arrive would be narcissus, or Chinese sacred lily, bulbs, which we placed in low bowls of water, the bulbs supported by the prettiest small white stones that the children could find. Just before New Year's Day, Ah Shee, Ah Key, and a few of our special friends began arriving with the other gifts--quantities of litchi nuts, candied fruits and cocoanut (sic), tangerines, chunks of sugar cane, jars of preserved ginger, and fireworks of all kinds. There were much more costly gifts, too, such as great squares of plain and brocaded silk to be used as handkerchiefs, umbrellas, Chinese slippers, fans, beautiful vases and bowls, figurines and hair ornaments.

When the big day of the celebration arrived, many people from Middletown, the nearest settlement, as well as all mine residents, were on hand to join in the festivities. For some reason, the fireworks were always set off in broad daylight in mid-afternoon, resulting in more noise than beauty. Long strings of dozens of bunches of firecrackers were hung by their fuses from poles, topped with figures of birds and beasts full of black powder. The string was lighted at the bottom, and after all of the firecrackers had exploded with a sharp sizzle, the powder went off with a terrifying roar. Bombs full of powder were also thrown, and rockets were sent up. An entry in my mother's diary one year says that "110,000 firecrackers and numerous bombs" were exploded. After the fireworks were over, the Chinese passed out gifts of nuts and candy to all the spectators. As a member of the family observes, such generosity, when their earnings were so meager, was something for even a small child to marvel at.

I am sure many of us older people have some of these lovely souveniers [sic] of long ago.

The Helen

...Actually, the mine consisted of two claims, patented in 1874, one under the name of Austin, the other under the name of Helen. After my parents, Andrew and Mary Rocca, bought the mine from two brothers, George and Thomas Wright in 1899, they gave it its third and final name, The Helen. In September 1900, my mother wrote a family friend: "We renamed the mine the 'Helen' after our dear little girl, now three-and-one-half years old." In all fairness, though, I think I must share the honors with that earlier and to me unknown Helen for whom one of the claims was named.

The Helen is in the Mayacamas quicksilver district or mountain range of California. It is situated at the head of the north branch of Dry Creek about 7 miles from Middletown, at an elevation of approximately 2,700 feet.

...All the tunnels at the Helen before 1900 had Spanish names--the San Juan, the Esperanza,... and the Santa Maria--and a shaft named the Mexican Cave. Of the ladders in this cave my brother, Andrew Rocca, Jr. wrote me, "They were just a pole with deep notches cut into it so that one could gain a foothold. In earlier days, the miners carried the ore up on their backs over these crude, insecure ladders."

...Nine of the Chinese who had worked for my father at the Great Western went with us to the Helen. Their first task was to reopen the old Santa Maria tunnel, then to try to bail water out of the shaft. The results were disheartening, since they were able to lower the water only 20 feet or a little over half the distance.

With discouraging results in two areas--failure to find the vein in the Long Tunnel, inability to drain the Santa Maria shaft--my parents seriously considered giving up the mine at that time. My mother had a great deal of faith in it, however, and it was she who persuaded my father to make one more try. Together they chose a location for a new tunnel, which they named the Beatrice Tunnel for their second daughter.

...The Chinese left the mine at the end of 1901 or early in 1902 and thereafter the underground work was done almost entirely by Italian miners. On August 1, 1902, the Cavagnero family, old friends of the Roccas from Great Western days, moved to the Helen and opened a boarding house for the Italian employees, a position they continued to hold for nearly twenty years.

...The Chinese passed from the scene at both the Great Western and the Helen mines in the early 1900s, being supplanted largely by Italian workmen. They and their shacks have long since vanished, but, as I have said, some of their work still stands in the fine timbering at the Great Western. Sometimes, too, deep down in the earth, even in modern times a miner chances upon a relic of the days when mining was done almost exclusively by the Chinese. When I last visited the Great Western in the 1930s, the man who owned the mine then told me that from time to time his workmen unearthed some memento of the Chinese--an article of wearing apparel generally, most often the tattered remains of what Julian Dana describes as their "huge, wide-brimmed, conical-tipped reed hats." But for those of us who knew them well, no such touching souvenir is necessary to keep green our tender memories of "the Chinamen."

Mountains
& Pioneers
of Lake County

Henry Mauldin

Lake County Historian

Mountains & Pioneers of Lake County

by Henry Mauldin, Lake County Historian
Edited by Carolyn Wing Greenlee
Cover: Stephanie C. Boyette
Copyright 1995 Carolyn Wing Greenlee
Published 1995 Earthen Vessel Productions

Mountain & Pioneers of Lake County
By Henry Mauldin, Lake County Historian

INTRODUCTION

In his twenty-seven years as historian of Lake County (1952-1979), Henry Mauldin wrote more than ten thousand type-written pages covering everything from geologic formations to stories and legends collected from historical sources and local longtime residents, many of whom were his personal friends.

One day when I was visiting the Lakeport museum, Curator Donna Howard said wistfully she wished stories from those pages could be made into books. I was into books. I loved stories. I was interested in pioneers, and curious about how places got their names. That became the book *Mountains & Pioneers of Lake County.*

Some of the stories were hard to believe, others tell of individuals and unusual circumstances that will remain for me forever connected with the places that bear their names.

MAHNKE PEAK

Mahnke Peak was given this name from the fact that the Mahnke family lived for 66 years one mile due north of the peak. John Mahnke was born in Hamburg, Germany in 1858 and went to Mexico in 1876, a well educated man speaking six languages, to work for a foreign office. There he married a native of that country in 1880 and prospered in his work.

He purchased a large ranch and entered into partnership with two others. Unknown to him, they tried several times to lead him into a death trap hoping that they would gain the property when he died.

In his line of work he was required to sign many papers, some so routine that he trusted those under him to take care of the details and relied on their judgment so he could sign without looking at the contents. One day some one slipped a special paper into a pile of these ordinary documents to be signed. This item, which he signed, was a statement whereby he took a stand against the Mexican government and was the same as signing his death warrant.

The signing of the document was effective and he, his wife and two children barely escaped with their lives, losing everything they had. In 1886 John Mahnke and his family came to San Francisco and on to Kelseyville where he worked at day labor and played the piano at resorts as he was an accomplished pianist and violinist…

In 1887 John Mahnke homesteaded and moved onto Stonebreaker Flat where he put up a log cabin. The only access was by a four mile trail over the ridge from Kelsey Creek Drive. All supplies were packed in by foot or mule and horse back. Over the years the children walked to school, a round trip of seven miles. … The family grew until it included nine children: Dan, Carolina, Clara, Emilio, Amanda, Enrique, Mabel, Mina and John…

About 1929 Enrique was hunting in the mountain area with a dog and gun on horseback. The dog jumped a wildcat and ran it under a manzanita bush. He got off the horse and started to get the gun out of the scabbard when the wildcat took off down the hill. To aid the dog in quietly tracking the animal he ran after it without his gun, thinking that after it was treed he would have time to go back and get his rifle. The wildcat ran down the hill into a briar patch and the hunter's momentum carried him down the hill into the brier patch where he stopped with the wildcat between his feet. In the excitement, with no time to think, he reached down, grabbed the wildcat and choked it to death. Luckily he had on gauntleted gloves and he never received a scratch.

Looking eastward from the summit of a gap as he journeyed from his port at Bodega Bay to his new hearthstone at Kushkoff, Captain Smith beheld afar o'er the rim of the eastern horizon, through another gap miles away, a noble, somber mountain standing—a lone sentinel of the vast, primeval empire behind and beyond it.

He had a sailing vessel down at yonder landing that had come to him from Russian ownership. On the bow was borne its name, "Saint Helena." It occurred to him that that was a fine sounding name, that he proceeded to bestow on the mountain that seemed an outpost between the wide interior of the continent and his far Pacific home.

From the *Californian,* July-December 1880
...quoted in the same book is a part of a speech by General Vallejo as given in Santa Rosa several years ago.

"In 1845, Governor Rotcheff advanced with a party of Russians to Mount Mayacmas, on the summit of which he affixed a brass plate bearing an inscription in his own language. He named the mountain St. Helena for his wife, the Princess de Gagarin. The beauty of the lady excited so ardent a passion in the breast of Prince Solano, chief of all the Indians about Sonoma, that he formed a plan to capture by force or stratagem the object of his love; and he might very likely have succeeded had I not heard of his intention in time to prevent its execution."

On June 12, 1841, Wosnessansky, a Russian naturalist attached to the Zoological Museum of St. Petersburg, ascended Mount Mayacama and placed a copper plate bearing an inscription in his native tongue, naming the mountain St. Helena.

Philip O'Neil was born at White Sulphur Springs, Miss., May 4, 1848. He came to California in 1851 where he grew up and became a fairly well educated man. Outside of the report that he was a San Francisco fireman, there is little known of his activities until he came to live at Castle Rock in 1889 where he set up a home for many years which he called "The Summit".

Work and Phil O'Neil never met. His only known occupation was as a professional gambler and a heavy drinker. His wife was a school teacher in the Bay area and a part of her salary plus a few dollars he won at cards kept him going.

While around San Francisco, between his drinking and gambling he got into trouble and it was necessary that he go somewhere else. His wife bought 120 acres including Castle Rock and the glades. Here Phil set up housekeeping alone, which he continued for several years. Not only did the glades take on the name by which they are still known, "O'Neil Openings", but also a peak on the ridge between the England Springs Toll Road and Mahnke Peak to the east, is known as O'Neil Peak. There is no known reason it should have been named after him except he was the nearest resident.

He never ceased going on a binge. Several times he got into trouble in our county, sometimes alone.

One time his wife had come up to visit him. It was summer and the flies were bad. When it came time for her to leave and

just before they left, she took many sheets of sticky fly paper—each sheet which was about 12 by 18 inches square—and laid them all over the bed. As that was the warm side of the house and the flies congregated there, she was thinking that by the time Phil got back most of the flies would have been caught by the sticky paper.

They left and she got on the stage at Kelseyville for the trip back to the city. Promptly he took on too much liquor and reached home after nightfall. In a hazy-eyed condition he took off all his clothes and lay down on top of the bed. He awoke next day all done up in fly paper, flies and all.

When the writer was a teenager, Phil O'Neil stopped several times for a neighborly meal. Generally this was followed by a friendly game of cards with no money involved. When asked why he always won he said he did this by cheating and practising [sic] the arts of his profession, that he would play no other way for fear he would get out of practise [sic]. He was a true Westerner and wore his hair long, coming to his shoulders.

Phil O'Neil moved in later years to a lower location on Adobe Creek and finally near Kelseyville where he passed on in the 1920s, a gambler, heavy drinker, but good natured (when sober) carefree individual to the last.

Both old toll roads over the Castle Rock pass are closed and abandoned for better routes. Phil O'Neil and his home are gone. Perhaps we cannot say we are proud to name O'Neil Openings and O'Neil Peak after him, but, for the sake of variety, why not?

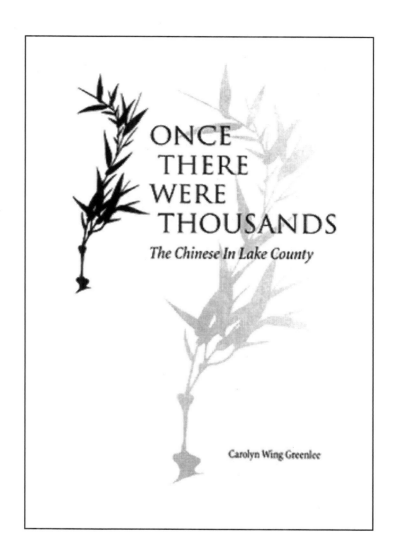

ONCE
THERE
WERE
THOUSANDS

The Chinese In Lake County

Carolyn Wing Greenlee

Once There Were Thousands

Stories from *The Life and Death of a Quicksilver Mine*
by Helen Rocca Goss used by permission
from the Andrew Rocca family
Stories from Norm Wilson told to Carolyn Wing Greenlee
used by permission of Norm Wilson
Cover: Stephanie C. Del Bosco

Once There Were Thousands
By Carolyn Wing Greenlee

INTRODUCTION

History. When I was going to school, it was the subject I disliked almost as much as algebra. History was dates of battles, lists of presidents, reigns of kings, treaties and significant events which bored me to death, and wars. Kingdoms rose and fell within a few pages, or even a few paragraphs. Time swept across my years of junior and senior high with broad strokes and, as one Russian film maker said, "people as caviar."

Then while I was working on a program with the Ontario Museum of History and Art, Director Theresa Hanley told me that history is now being considered in terms of agency. People are individuals who make choices. It is no longer a matter of governments whooshing through lands knocking over everything in their way. It is no longer lists of dates and names. History is made of people choosing to do or not do, stay or not stay. Their choices become history.

Another thing I've learned: history is not absolute, infallible Truth. History depends on who is doing the telling. World War II looks quite different, I'm sure, to the Japanese. History is biased—sometimes, because people are pushing their programs, sometimes because people have to choose what of the myriad of details will be organized into some sort of order for presentation to the public—an attempt, as all storytellers do, to make sense of what happened and why, and to identify its significance and meaning.

For ample, if you are writing on the California Gold Rush, will you choose to focus only on the men because you feel there were too few women to make a difference in the total picture? Or will you document each woman's story believing that she is too significant to leave out? Historian and author JoAnn Levy said the more

85

rare something is, the more value it has. That's why she searched in the archives and found enough gold rush women to fill a book: *They Saw Elephants.*

Was it worth the effort? What could be known by delving into diaries, letters, eye-witness accounts? To her surprise, JoAnn found that not all women went West kicking and screaming. Some went for adventure, and a number of them did quite well in the Wild Wild West. Was this previously unpublished information significant enough to change the total picture? For me it was. It spurred me to search the accounts of my own silent kinsmen. How would my present concepts of them and the society that hated them be modified by a more detailed and fundamental detection ?

I had lived in Lake County for sixteen years before I ever heard that there had once been Chinese living here. Jim, a volunteer at the Lakeport Museum, mentioned he had seen a pair of tiny embroidered shoes in a box in storage and then I recalled seeing a battered red drum in a corner of the old Schoolhouse Museum Lower Lake. I began looking through the Mauldin accounts and the book Curator Donna Howard made sure I read, *The Life and Death of a Quicksilver Mine* by Helen Rocca Goss. The evidence was plentiful and eye opening. Chinese had worked in the mines, built toll roads, grown vegetables down in Lower Lake where the water was good, served as cooks and servants in homes, and managed stores. Main Street Lower Lake had Chinese laundries and restaurants.

During the time before Middletown or Clearlake Oaks, when stage coach drivers reined their steaming horses to a halt in Lower Lake and almost every place else was vast, uncultivated land, the Chinese came to work—hundreds of them. Without Mauldin's carefully collected accounts and the meticulously documented details in the book by Helen Rocca Goss, the Chinese of Lake County would have remained invisible—gone without a trace except for the battered red drum in the corner of the Old Schoolhouse Museum and the tiny embroidered shoes in the storage box in Lakeport.

Even though I am not publishing *Once There Were Thousands,* my book on the Chinese of the area, it was worth all the work to find that their story is not merely the record of unprecedented hatred directed at one specific race during a time of enormous need for cheap labor. I now have indisputable eye-witness proof, though rare, of people who recognized the Chinese as fellow human beings whose lives mattered and whose contributions made a difference in the life that flowed from what they did. It is an addition to California history which, without it, is not completely the truth.

Helen Rocca Goss was born smack in the midst of that ugly period of American history. Her accounts of her father's dealings with the workers at the quicksilver mines appear earlier in this book. Here, however, I include her own stories of certain Chinese who served around their household.

The other stories in this section are from California State Archaeologist Norm Wilson. I met Norm in Auburn, California, when I was invited to help document and explore the newly re-opened joss house, as it was called back then. In the course of many conversations, Norm told me stories of his father, an example of individual agency at its best. I don't know if Norm wrote his stories down or told them to anyone else, so here they are, to honor my very special friend, his father, and their legacy of free thinking, that they might never be forgotten.

My Dad and the Cook at the Jarvis Mine
by Norm Wilson

My dad, Ward Wilson, was never one to be racially prejudiced. He worked a lot with Blacks in the shipyards in World War II. His father was a pioneer in Kansas. Came as a Free Stater. Moved from Maine to help. Then went to Idaho, Oregon, and California. My family can be traced back to the 16th and 17th century (including Hugunots). They've always been sort of rebellious against people telling them what to do.

My dad was a Westerner. He grew up where they had to cut the mustard, in the mines or anything else. He worked along side many kinds of people. He always said they had to prove themselves.

In the '30s in Forest Hills Divide, my dad was working at Jarvis Mine. They had a Chinese cook. The cook was very important in those days. If you don't have good food, the men will leave. He was a good cook. He made all the things the men liked. I was a little boy at the time, and he'd sneak things out to me sometimes—a little potatoes or a piece of pie. He was very Anglo in his cooking.

My dad ate with the men. The cook would always set the food in front of him. Then my dad would divvy it up. The cook would bring the different dishes and always set it at the head of the table in front of my dad to give him the honor. Often dessert would be an apple pie. My dad would always ask him to bring the ketchup to pour on the pie. The cook would go into a tirade saying, "What's a matter you!" It was a little running joke between them.

One time there was a bear that was coming around and starting to break into things. The cook asked the men at the mine to get him. Nobody did. They told him not to worry, but the cook didn't want the bear breaking into things. After a while, the cook said we didn't have to worry about the bear anymore. I said, "What happened?" He took me out behind the building and I saw the bear lying there dead. He said he had been leaving the bear an apple every night on the back stairs. So after the bear was used to getting an apple every night, the cook pushed some dynamite capsules into an apple and left it for him. The bear came for the apple, took a big bite and blew his head off.

My dad thought it was pretty neat because he'd never heard of anyone doing such a thing before. I know my dad really liked this man.

HELP AROUND THE HOUSE
BY HELEN ROCCA GOSS

Another more amusing Chinese who sometimes helped with the gardening was Ah Quan, a very small man whose English was limited to one or two half-sentences. As Ah Quan labored patiently among the roses and chrysanthemums, my oldest sister writes:

When he grew weary of nursemaiding, out would come one of his two English sentences, repeated again and again: "Your Mama callee you." Like most of the outdoor workers, he carried liquid refreshments, which we children were diplomatically taught to regard as cold tea. It was probably some kind of Chinese wine, and it was in a lovely urn-shaped pottery jug. These discarded brown jars made handsome bud vases and, if available, would be correct anywhere today.

For a time Ah Quan worked nine and one-half hours a day, leaving his work half an hour early to do the cooking, or some of it, for his China camp. He received an extra ten cents a day for his culinary efforts--a total of $1.35. In addition to cooking, his duties included buying some of the supplies from the mine store. Ah Quan was one of the brightest of the Chinese, and he knew the English names of only a few articles. To avoid forgetting his errand before he reached his destination, he would sing the items over and over as he walked along. Kerosene was usually at the top of his list, and the whole camp became familiar with Ah Quan's favorite theme song--"Littee-bitee-coalee-oilee," repeated dozens of times. He was one of the nine Chinese who went with us to the Helen Mine in 1900, and there, too, he was the errand boy, coming to our home at regular intervals to get kerosene. Because I was a small child when we left the Great Western, my memories of the Chinese are largely from the early 1900s at the Helen Mine. One such memory stands out sharply--playing outdoors in the still twilight of a warm summer evening and hearing Ah Quan approach. At first there was just a faint, muffled sound in the canyon far below us as he set out on his mission, then as he climbed up the steep trail and came nearer, the words of his cheerful but monotonous little song became distinguishable -- "Littee-bitee-coalee-oilee." Finally, a tiny, gnome-like figure emerged over the brow of the hill below us, and there was Ah Quan, smiling happily if somewhat vacantly, holding out his empty kerosene can and still intoning his bit of sing-song....

Among those who acted as servants in our home, Ah Date was outstanding and he was with us off and on for many years. In earlier times, however, there had been another Chinese servant, Ah Sam, whose specialty was unusually crisp pop-overs, which he served again and again. After he had worked for the family some years, he went away, returning for a brief stay two or three years later. Those were the days of the tong wars, and it was always assured that fear of either the tong or the law was responsible for his sudden departure. In any case, one morning about nine o'clock he went back to the China camp for a few moments. He returned to his post in the kitchen, but as soon as the noonday meal was on the stove, he announced that "Cousin sick," and nothing could deter him from rushing off to catch the outbound stage connecting with the San Francisco train.

Ah Date was the cook in our home whenever other help was not available, but he much preferred to work underground. He was an enormous eater, however, and his fondness for pork chops, thick juicy steaks, and similar delicacies was all that reconciled him to his long tours of kitchen duty. Mother had taught him to cook, and the plain cooking he did was very good, though rather monotonous, since he confined himself to a few standard dishes, served all too frequently. Still, he was capable of some surprise menus. One evening his mistress asked him to make hot cakes for breakfast, forgetting that she had not taught him how to make them. To the astonishment of everyone, Date served plain cake, hot from the oven, for breakfast the following morning. Always dressed in a clean white blouse with his queue plastered on the back of his head, Date was immaculate, and he kept his kitchen so, too. The last thing he did every evening was to scrub the kitchen floor, even if his other work was not finished until as late as 10 o'clock.

...Date was not fond of children, and when we were guilty of too much intrusion, he discouraged further advances by looking very stern and sharpening intently a large butcher knife.

Inside

the

Oy

Quong

Laundry

a memoior of
Kathleen Kong Wing

Kathleen Kong Wing with
Carolyn Wing Greenlee

Inside the Oy Quong Laundry
a memoir of Kathleen Kong Wing

Copyright 1995 Kathleen Kong Wing
and Carolyn Wing Greenlee
Cover: Daniel Worley
Cover photo: Carolyn Wing Greenlee
Published 1995 Earthen Vessel Productions

Inside the Oy Quong Laundry
By Kathleen Kong Wing with Carolyn Wing Greenlee

Introduction

All my life I had heard the same bitter stories—the eight-year-old child struggling to press endless baskets of other people's clothes with a heavy sadiron heated on a coal-burning stove. Eventually I tuned them out, but when I grew up I realized my mother had actually lived inside a proverbial Chinese laundry and I began to ask her to tell me more. "Why?" my mother snarled. "Don't waste your time. Nobody cares."

"But I do," I said. She didn't believe me. Growing up in Central California in the 1920s, Mom was considered a worthless Chinese, and in Chinese culture, she was a worthless female. In both worlds it had been made quite clear: her life was inconsequential. Nobody cared.

Then my father was confined to bed. During that time I began transcribing tapes of stories he was telling about his childhood. Mom overheard them and began remembering some of her own. She became more willing to answer my questions, and when I edited and read them back to her, she was genuinely interested. Slowly she started to believe I really did want to know, and to realize perhaps she had something worth telling.

Over the months, I saw my mother's childhood through her adult eyes focused now with understanding that comes only with the passage of many years. At first there were more bitter stories, then a mixture of horrors and adventures, and then insights and observations and even beauties noticed with wonder by a child with a sensitive and artistic heart. I never would have guessed.

When I returned home, Mom started calling me often. "I remembered something," she would say, and she'd relate a story that was interesting or funny or lovely—such as the screen bed her father made for the kids to sleep outside on hot summer nights.

It healed her. Telling her stories healed her. Someone had cared to ask, listen, and write them down. Someone thought her sorrows were worth remembering. They would not be lost, her cries going unheard in the din of suffering humanity.

My mother always said everyone has a story, but she had never considered her own of any worth until I valued them enough to listen. Then, as if they had been lanced, seventy-three years of memories poisoned by bitter struggles and sorrows drained away. She became a different person.

Of the forty or so books I have written or edited, *Inside the Oy Quong Laundry* is still my favorite. I love my mother's voice, and I love the healing that came as she spoke her truth.

When she was terribly ill only a few years later, I had the joy of bringing a tape of the book for my mother to hear. The Talking Books organization in Sacramento had found a copy of *Oy Quong Laundry* in the State Library and chose to turn it into an audio book for the blind. I found out because the volunteer who was doing the reading called me to ask how to pronounce the *Sam Yup*. Since I subscribed to Talking Books, I ordered a copy of the tape and played it for my mom, propping the big yellow player on her bed. We listened to the entire thing nonstop.

Mom lay hearing her words read in another woman's voice. It sounded like a real book. Afterwards, she was quiet, but her eyes were glowing. Though by then she couldn't talk well, she managed to croak out something that made me know she was pleased—with the reading, with the book, with her story. She knew she was dying, but what a wonderful gift to leave behind! She had found wisdom in the bitter places and now she could give it to everyone who read her book. Legacy beyond your lifetime is the gift of your story to the world.

Kathleen: If everything you had was sweet, it wouldn't be enjoyable. You need a contrast. You might want some salt or a little pepper or *foo gua*. But do you know?—I like *foo gua*. It's bitter when you're eating it, but afterwards you can feel a *herng* flavor.

It leaves a good taste. I guess when you've experienced the bitter, after the bitter is over, it leaves you with a good feeling. Like eating *foo gua*—that was my life inside the Oy Quong Laundry.

foo gua: bitter melon
herng: fragrance in the mouth, a lovely aftertaste

IMMIGRANTS

Watching the Super IMAX feature "Alaska," I was overwhelmed by the sight of salmon leaping vertically up a giant waterfall six stories high. How tiny they seemed! How impossible their task! The scene changed to show eggs magnified so large they filled the screen. The narrator said they would develop and grow "in water enriched by their parents' decomposing bodies."

Water
  pounds
   straight
    down.
  Home lies
  straight up.
Against such
  rush & crash
you fling yourself
       past rocks
         bears
       exhaustion
        flailing air
          gasping
       iridescence gone
         no glory left
           save one:
          this I do
           for my young

The place where we ironed was also the front room where we did business with the public. We were open seven days a week. Since we lived there, it didn't matter because we were doing other things when we weren't taking care of customers. And even though we worked long hours, the parents were always right there so we felt secure.

The front door was solid wood with a window in it. We also had a screen door. When we were done for the day, we'd shut the doors and pull the shades down on the door and the two front windows. That meant we were closed. I used to dream about those doors. Did I shut both of them? I guess I didn't want anyone to come in after we shut up for the night.

Our customers were known by the kinds of laundry they brought in. There was one fellow who used to bring in, with the rest of his laundry, socks that smelled dreadfully. So he was known as Stinky Socks. Another person who brought things in always had two towels. He was known as Two Towels. Each one of these different customers that had things that were constant had been dubbed by the description of their laundry. When they'd come in to pick up their things, the guy would holler, "Here comes ol' Stinky Socks!" Of course, the customers never caught on because it was all in Chinese.

The ironing boards were pieces of rectangular wood covered with cloth for padding. Pop made the ironing boards. I used to climb up on the ironing board and look out the window at the rain. That was wonderful. When the street was wet and the raindrops would hit, they would sprout up and look to me like little water plants.

When it rained, we made little paper boats. The paper boats are made like the paper hats. You'd put it in the gutter in the street and it would float down on the rain water that was flowing down so fast. We'd run alongside on the sidewalk, trying to keep up. It was fun.

On top of the side stove there was a rack where the irons heated. It had eight sides and there were eight irons. Each of the flat sides had a little rack on the bottom. You'd take the eight-pound iron and sit them on these little racks so the flat plate would be against the stove. The stove is burning hot coals in there and it heats up the iron. Then you get this big pot holder that was round. It was permanently bent so it would fit around the handle of the iron. You'd pick up one and put it on the big eight-pound flat iron. You never touched the handle of the iron with your bare hand.

You'd get so you could feel how hot the iron is. If it's been there too long, it's too hot and will burn the clothes, so you'd hook the handle of the iron with a long wire and dip it in a bucket of water to cool it off a little bit. Then you took it out and ironed holding the iron with the big round bent pot holder. I started when I was eight years old. That's the reason I've got these tremendous-sized shoulders. Imagine! Eight pounds all day long! It was like weight lifting.

Sometimes the women customers washed their own clothes, but they didn't want to iron them so they brought them in to us. Those clothes required more care and had to be ironed on a little ironing board like the ones we use now. When I was about twelve, my mom said, "You do it. You do it better than I do." I guess I took more pains with the lacy stuff. So I had to do all the intricate blouses. Whenever the work came in of that sort, I had to put the ironing board up in the little space between the two ironing boards and the shelf and iron the blouses and shirts. Ten cents apiece. Later they got me a newfangled electric iron. No thermostatic control. If it got too hot, I had to unplug it and wait for it to cool down. When it got too cool, I had to plug it in again.

When I was five or six years old, they had me turn the socks. I put them together in pairs. At eight, I was doing the ironing. Mom and Pop were very busy with the laundry, so they also had me do the cooking. I made the rice in the big wok. Imagine eight year-olds carrying those big woks! The rice left a crust in the bottom. I'd put water on it and it'd soak. Then I'd clean it up and the chickens got the rice.

Well, one day, the water was in the wok in preparation to cleaning it out and taking it to the chickens. My father came in and says, "Time to make lunch." I said, "I don't want to! I'm tired of cooking! I'm tired of working! I'm working all the time!" Big. Loud. The way I usually am. He didn't say anything. He just went over to the wok. The rice was already soaking. He scooped the rice into a bowl. I guess he must have put soy sauce and oil in it and ate it. He just looked at me, so hurt. I never did it again. Never! I realized that if I didn't do it, he wouldn't get anything to eat. They were so busy they didn't have time to cook. So I never said I wouldn't cook again. I cooked.

GUTTING CHICKENS

I took over the kitchen by the time I was eight, but I didn't have to do all the things. If I had the chicken to cook, it was all plucked and the insides were all cleaned out. Then, afterwards, I learned to pluck them. Then, as soon as I learned to pluck them, my mom would say, "You pluck the chickens." So I plucked the chickens. They had to be scalded and then the feathers came out.

Then one day I said, "Well, they're so busy, I think I'll go pull out the insides." So I did the incision and I put my hands in and I went, "AKKKK!" Still warm! Yucky! The chicken was newly dead. Still warm inside. I pulled all the insides out. Yuck! I didn't want to do it anymore. Mom said, "Oh, that was good. Now cook it." She was always matter-of-fact. No praise. No anything. Just do it. And I did. I cooked it. The next time she had a chicken, I plucked it. Mom says, "Clean it up and cook it." I said, "I don't want to do it! Every time I learn something, you make me do it." That's when I learned a lesson. She told me, "When you learn it, it's yours."

I now know how to pull the insides out of a chicken. I remember that as a lesson. If I learned it, even if I had to do it, I learned it while somebody was there to teach it. So they teach me and I still don't like it—I still will learn it. Then, if I need it, I will already know it. See? That has been one of the things throughout my whole life. Learn what I have to. I still learn everything I can on everything. And then it's mine.

Learning is a good thing even if it's painful. It's like hitting yourself on the head with a hammer. It's so nice when you quit. But you will have learned. When you hit yourself on the head with a hammer, you've learned something. Isn't that true? But I guess a lot of people can give that same kind of teaching to their kids a little less painful—"Do it!" So I did. From then on, I had to do chicken. But to their credit, they never made me kill it. I don't think I could kill it. I still don't.

THE LOVE OF DAD

My father used to bring me presents once in a while. One time he brought me a big beautiful box—dark stained wood with carvings all over and a brass Chinese clasp. I think he did it because he knew I had to work so hard and he wanted to make up for it. Pop didn't talk much. He did things that let you know he loved you.

Then one day my dad brought me a great big doll. I live with my guilt every time I think about it. It was a great big, scrawny, floppy doll. You know me. I look at the expressions on the faces. Even now, when I look at dolls or stuffed animals, I always look at their faces. I have to love the little thing. And to me that big floppy doll was the ugliest thing I ever saw. My father bought it for me with all the love in his heart and I said, "It's ugly! I don't want it!" and flung it away. It laid there in the yard in the dirt, an unloved and unclaimed doll. It never found a home. I can see my father's face today. Forever, I have always been ashamed of myself, but I could not undo. The only thing you can say—I was a very young child.

I hurt my father twice—the doll and the rice. That's the only times, but I can still feel the hurt in his eyes. He never hurt anybody in his life. Anybody that hurt him is a rat. And I'm a rat. He never raised his voice. He never said anything against anybody. Never criticized. Never reprimanded us. He just loved us and was standing there for us. Have you ever seen the strong guy standing there being strong for you, and you felt comforted that he was there for you? That's what he was like.

When I was about eight, I had diphtheria. I went to the county hospital and stayed in one of the cabins along the side. Each cabin was for a different communicable disease. A fence was there to keep people from being exposed to the germs. My dad would come to the fence and talk to me through the window. My father was not very verbal, and all I could see was the longing in his face and his frustration of not being able to get close.

I was in the Pest House two weeks. I can remember the longing of the little kid wanting to go home with the parent. It must have been around Christmas because one of the night nurses brought me a book, The Night Before Christmas, and read it to me. Later on when I was by myself, I'd flip through it. It was my only book. But I had to leave it when I left. I couldn't take it home because it was polluted with germs.

Awhile ago, I bought a great big copy of that story. It's in the bookcase in Tom's study. I wondered, why did I buy it? Then I remembered. To this day, that book is very special to me. It still reminds me of the kindness of the night nurse.

One time my dad took me to get some shoes. There was a little Jewish shoe store on 16th Street which was a skid row-type of thing. It didn't have the greatest things in the world, but there was this pair of shoes that I bought. It didn't fit. My feet were painful and I was hobbling, but we didn't have a lot of money so I didn't say anything. My dad said, "What's the matter?" I said, "Well, the shoes hurt my feet." He didn't say a word. He took me by the hand

and went back to the store and bought me another pair of shoes that fit. He took the other pair and said, "We throw these away." That was great understanding because anybody that throws away a pair of shoes, my gosh! That was my dad that did that for me.

Once I was playing hop scotch with the neighborhood kids. They were taking a rock and breaking glass to make the thing that you throw in the squares. One of the pieces of glass flew up and hit my eye. I ran home and told my parents, "They threw the rock and broke the glass and it cut my eye!" They rushed me to the hospital, but the doctor said it was beyond his ability. He recommended a doctor in Modesto. Pop didn't know English, and I didn't know much either, so he got the information written on a piece of paper.

That night, my dad carried me to the bus station, caught the Greyhound Bus and took me to Modesto. I was very motion sick. When we arrived, I got sick on the lawn. Then my dad carried me into the hospital. I must have fallen asleep because, the next thing I knew, I woke up in the hospital. They had operated on my eye. I had a patch over it. I stayed there for a month. In those days, they kept you a long time.

Medicine was very different back then. They wouldn't let us get up even to use the bathroom, so we had to use bedpans, but the day nurse growled at me every time I asked for one. She flung herself around and scared me. I was very little. It got so every time I needed a bed pan I'd cry because I was afraid of her.

There were two other ladies in the room. They were nice. When I cried, they would ring and ask the nurse to bring me the bedpan. She didn't growl at them. The day nurse was so mean she made me cry. But I think the Lord had me cry. They didn't have antiseptic back then, and the tears kept the eye clean. The night nurse was very nice. She brought me little toys, little people. I'd push the figurines around on my tray.

My dad came to see me once a week. Every week he got on the bus in Merced and came all the way. Visit and go home. It was hard on them, taking time off work. I don't know if it was hard on my mom. She was the one who had to stay home. Couldn't close the laundry. Sometimes it's harder not knowing.

The fourth week, he took me home. They dressed me, but when I tried to stand up, my legs wouldn't hold me. I collapsed. So my dad carried me. We got on the bus and went home. The first thing my mom said to me was, "You are so expensive!" It cost $200 in the 1920s. That was a lot of money.

The Screen Bed

One time, my dad made us a screen bed outside in the Dry Yard under the wires of the clotheslines. I don't know whose idea it was. A lot of times it's Mom's ideas, but Pop was always the one who, with no training, gets his little old ruler and his plane and his hammer and his nails and a saw and he'd build the different things—not as a finished carpenter might, but adequate enough.

It was just like a chicken cage—four sides and a roof of aluminum or metal screening that the mosquitoes can't come in. There's lots of mosquitoes in Merced! And a solid wood bottom. It was off the ground on little legs—legs high enough so we couldn't climb in. I don't know how high it was. To a little child, it looked real tall. We were small then. That was in the old laundry days. We got along real good. Gee, we didn't fight or anything.

They must have thrown a cotton linter double mattress in there (it looked awfully big) and they picked the four of us up and put us in there—Walter, Marilyn, Katie, and me. They shut the little door and we slept outside under the stars. It's so hot in Merced, night and day, so we didn't need blankets or anything.

One time we looked out there and we saw shooting stars. They had some big ones, like big balls of fire, shoot from one horizon to the other. We'd go "Wow!" Very appreciative. They were all the time, big ones and little ones every few minutes. Every minute or so—stars and stars until we finally fell asleep. It was the most wonderful experience I had.

It took me to old age to find out what I saw as a child in the screen bed. I read about it. It was the Perseid meteor shower which happens as Earth passes through the tail of a comet. I went out other times and looked and looked in vain. Only in August were there star showers.

In August, every August, it comes. It usually starts around ten or eleven at night—magnificent shooting stars! Sometimes it gives you a thrill—goes *whoooom!* clear across the sky! It was just outstanding going to sleep under the stars safe in our yard.

The Uncle That Gambled

Kay: My mom told me we used to have seventeen workers at the laundry. That was before my time. Maybe it was when they had the old hand-laundry, because by the time I was old enough to remember, they only had one helper. He worked for my dad for years. We called him Uncle. He wasn't a real uncle—just someone from the same village. He lived with us. I was terrible to him. He insisted on playing his Chinese records every Sunday. I didn't have many records—maybe two—but I wanted to hear mine, not his. I'd play my music as loud as he would play his music. Today, I would say I would have deserved it if my dad had swatted me. I was a brat. Maybe I would have been less of a brat now if he had done it then, but he didn't. So every Sunday there was "Red River Valley" loudly competing with the Chinese music that Uncle wanted to hear.

My father paid his workers. He would be banker for them. He had this famous chest underneath the bed that they put all their valuables in—their jewels and their money and everything. They didn't trust the bank. Banks were not very trustworthy in those days. They didn't have FDIC so the people just kept their money in the house somewhere.

Well, this uncle worked and worked and worked. He had $200 that he left with my father. I don't know how many years he worked, but they didn't make very much in those days. Very low pay. Anyway, he wanted his money. My father says, "No. Let me keep your money for you—safe for you so when you go home you will have this money." "Home" means "go to the Orient" because, in those days, all the old fellows that came over here left their wives at home. Then, when they made their money, they would go home. But the man insisted, so my dad gave him his money. In less than two hours, he was back—green. He had lost it all.

He lost it gambling at Mr. Wong's place. Mr. Wong was the richest guy in town. He had a two-story house and a car. Wow! That was largess! And a telephone! He and his wife had five children and they chose prominent white city persons to be godmother to this one and godfather to that one. He was one of those we call "Rice Christians"—'cause they weren't sincere about Christianity, they were just using it to their advantage. When they weren't at the Catholic Church, they were at the Buddhist Temple, and they would light the punk (incense) or whatever they did in those places. People used to laugh and say, "They're over there at the temple." But for the sake of their position in the town, they were always good Catholics too.

The people who owned the gambling places were the rich guys because all the Chinese people were not smart enough to stay away from gambling. They have a thing for gambling, and they're so poor. As Tom would say, they were so poor they hoped that somehow one of them would be rich enough to get out of the hole that they're all in. They'd never seen huge wealth. And if they see somebody else win, they think, "Oh, there's no reason it can't be me."

When I say to people, "I will never win the lottery," they say to me, "Oh, have faith. You'll get it!" I say, "No, I won't ever win 'cause I don't ever buy any." I don't buy lottery tickets so, naturally, I'm not going to win. No throwing good money after that. I work hard for my money. I'd rather have the dollar and use it for some other good cause. Like Tom. Every time he sees those people at Christmastime, he can't go past without putting money in their buckets. That dollar goes better.

Anyway, that uncle lost everything. It happened to so many! Eventually he got enough money to go home, but broke. In those days, $200 was a lot of money. In the 1920s, you could almost get a house for it. So the uncle went back to China. He probably felt horrible. In those days, everybody had to go home and show off how much they had. He felt bad, but I bet they were glad to have him home.

NEW YEARS PRINCESS

Once in a while when it got too bad in Merced, my mom and dad would go to San Francisco to have a little social life. They got tired of small town. No culture. Catch the cab to the railroad station. Take a ride. Check in at the hotel. Mom would have dinner with the ladies and carry on the gossip—who's got a new baby and whose child got married—you know. Sometimes I'd get to go, too. My mom loved these Chinese operas. The woman would stand there and sing two hours straight nonstop. Everybody is eating handfuls of watermelon seeds, biting them and spitting, and I'm biting them and watching.

The only thing I remembered out of the Peking Opera was that one of the women came out with a black *cherong sam*. It was beautifully embroidered with brilliantly colored butterflies of all sizes and shapes going from the hem of her dress, diagonally up over one shoulder, and down across the back. I just loved it. I've always dreamed of it. I always thought, "That is so beautiful! Someday I'll have a black dress with butterflies embroidered on it." The butterflies were jewel-like against the black silk background. Not shiny silk. Matte silk with all these colorful butterflies just glowing. All different colors, shapes, and sizes. I can always remember front and back! Not just front. Front and back. That's the only thing I can remember of the Peking Opera. And the seeds. And boring. Worse than boring.

The costumes were spectacular, though. Once I got to wear one just like in the opera. When I was thirteen, there was a big New Year's parade. Mr. Wong, who had a gambling house, asked me to be the princess. They said I would wear fancy clothes and ride a horse through the streets. I had never been on a horse, but they

107

said, "You don't have to worry. All you have to do is sit on the horse and look pretty. Two Boy Scouts will lead the horse through the streets." So I said okay.

The costume was gorgeous—layers and layers and layers of luxurious fabrics. I had to be dressed by professionals from San Francisco who knew how to dress that kind. It had great big wings with flags flapping—very heavy—and a great big headdress with pompoms and pheasant feathers—also very heavy. There were mirrors and pieces of metal sewed in which added to the weight. When I walked, I would clank and shine, clank and shine. So they dressed me and lifted me up to sit on the horse, who could tell right away that I didn't know how to ride.

When we started off, we walked along pretty good with the Boy Scouts leading the horse, and that was nice. But then they threw a whole string of firecrackers under the horse. The horse and I, neither one, were used to firecrackers under our feet. It started standing up on its hind legs. I grabbed the horn of the saddle and hung on for dear life. They kept throwing strings of firecrackers under the horse the whole way. It kept rearing and pitching. The Boy Scouts could barely keep it under control. I was scared. I felt very unprincess-like. I bet they were sorry they put me on the horse. I must have looked pretty grim.

Both the horse and I were glad when the parade was over. When they took it home, it probably ran into the barn and hid.

The Boys at Lincoln Market

There were a lot of young boys who came in to work for Mom and Pop at Lincoln Market. They were juvenile delinquents, Chinese-style, which meant they were straying, but by Chinese standards which, by American standards, was not very far. Probably in *fook,* which was filial piety which was involved in taking care of family and old people—the most important thing in the substance of family life. The relatives knew there was a place to put their wayward boys because my parents had big hearts and were very strict in right and wrong. The boys could learn a trade and be around good people, and they'd straighten out.

If you are a good example, the children see it. It was like learning a language. If everyone is speaking Spanish, anything else you speak would be totally different from what the others were speaking. If you're around good, hard-working, honest people, your bad behavior sticks out like a sore thumb.

Many young boys came, worked at the market, grew up, and went off and new ones came. They learned a trade—how to be butchers and grocery men. My mom was a surrogate mother. They were always at our house for Christmas or New Years. The other times they lived in the dorm that my father built for them. It was really a controlled environment. Go to work. Go to school. Come back to work. The food was provided for them and the dorm. They didn't get into trouble. They all straightened out and they all worked hard. They took their skills back with them and every one of them opened their own grocery store and became quite successful. We sure proliferated the grocery stores around! They all had the example of hard work, too, and they worked hard in their markets. They bought houses and had income and it was just wonderful. It shows you how two good people could change so many lives for the good.

"Fascinating, stunning, compelling!"
—Elizabeth Swan, Guide Dogs for the Blind

Steady Hedy

A Journey through Blindness & Guide Dog School

Carolyn Wing Greenlee

Steady Hedy
A Journey through Blindness & Guide Dog School

Steady Hedy
By Carolyn Wing Greenlee

INTRODUCTION

A Google search for America's #1 most feared disability brings up vision loss and a long list of research and published articles to back it up. One study revealed that some people who never suffered from depression or suicidal tendencies actually killed themselves. Why? You lose your independence. You lose your privacy. You lose your job. You lose your sense of who you are and what you're worth.

I had been a professional photographer for thirty years, a prolific writer and researcher. Suddenly I couldn't read, much less see what was in my viewfinder. Suddenly I was pathetically handicapped, dependent, landlocked, all my freedoms gone. I had lost my work, my direction, my ability to drive, even my sense of myself. What was the point of even trying? Everything was frustrating. Even plugging something into the wall was an ordeal.

When I struggled through the two years covered in this book, I had no idea that my reactions to my loss were so typical, or so dangerous. It would have been far too easy to quit trying—except there were dedicated people who would not let me lie down in the snow and go to sleep, so to speak. They directed me to solid ground and encouraged me to plant my feet upon it.

Lots of people have gone blind. Lots of people have had to deal with cancer or dementia, divorce, the death of a child. Lots of people took the overland trails. It helps to know many have made it through ahead of you, but you still have to find your own way. You have to discover what makes you want to stay and build a new life in an unfamiliar place. I think one thing that makes it better is believing it will be worth the work. Something good will come from the hardships, sufferings, and frightening unknowns—that

God can still birth life from the pain and somehow work it all together for Good.

If you had asked me at the beginning why I was writing this book, I would have said, "I want people to know how it felt to thrash through my blindness, and what it was like to be behind the walls of a guide dog school." But now I say it's about how our worst nightmares can become the source of our greatest healing. Every time I worked through another edit, I received new insight into the significance of ordinary occurrences. It was surprising and encouraging. I think most of us have such busy schedules that we don't take time to read our lives. We miss the deep blessings of the mundane, the daily devine.

My counselor Dr. Susan Hirshfield said, "You can fight the blindness, it will exhaust you and you will lose, or you can embrace it and see what happens." What happened was—and continues to be—some of the best change in my life.

Whether you're facing your own terrifying plunge into darkness or are simply satisfying your curiosity about the guide dog experience, I pray your eyes will be opened to the divine intervention in the details of your life—show you its meaning, its potential, and the beauty that lies just out of sight, waiting to be found.

FINDING SEARS

Irma was frantic. She needed a pair of dressier slacks for the portrait of her and her guide dog that was scheduled for Wednesday evening. We were all surprised when we found out it was going to be soon. We decided we needed to go to the mall. They told us it was easy to find. It was just over there.

After relieving our dogs and putting them on tie down in our rooms, we had an hour to find the mall that was "just over there," shop for pants for Irma, and make it back before dinner. We found Kathy Kelly and told her know we were going to the mall.

Chelsie saw us heading out with our canes and said she wanted to come. Precious time was ticking away. While Chelsie was putting her dog on tie down and getting her cane, we told Kathy that

Chelsie was going with us. Kathy said, "Okay, but I'm going off shift. You'll have to tell Stephanie." So then we had to find Stephanie, who was just coming on shift. Stephanie said okay and asked that we let her know when we got back.

The three of us set out across the campus, found the gift shop, the paths, the gate. Chelsie had pretty good night vision. Irma had good directional sense. I didn't have any special talents, so I just cheered us on. I had never gone on a night walk in a city to an unfamiliar place with two other blind people. The three of us were hurrying along with our canes in the dimming light.

After some wandering, Irma found the mall. It was big. Right in front was Sears. We flew past the big glass doors and followed Chelsie (who was an expert shopper) to the women's clothes department where we milled around the way you'd expect low vision people to mill when they have no idea where anything is and there's no one around to help. But time was short. We couldn't waste it. Irma found a sales lady named Christine who not only steered us to the right stuff, she stuck around to answer questions and offer guidance and opinions. Thus Irma quickly found the pants she needed.

It was pitch black by the time we left Sears—some street lights, but a lot of dark. We caned little arcs in front of us as we hurried through the parking lot. It didn't look right. Irma noticed first. We backtracked. We called directions back and forth—conjectures of which direction to turn. We giggled. It was fun even when we ran into one another.

We followed Chelsie whose eye problem did not include severe night blindness, Irma giving directions, and me behind laughing and having a wonderful time. It was suspenseful because we had to get back or miss dinner. It was fun because we were out in the dark fumbling along and the worst that could happen was we'd miss dinner. We found the narrow sidewalk and the black metal gate that led back into the grounds of Guide Dogs for the Blind. "How do we get it open?" Nobody knew. "Is it locked?" We couldn't find a lock. We couldn't find a latch. "Where's the handle?" Our fingers were feeling around where logic told us something mechanical should be. None of us remembered how we got it open when we left.

I thought, *Maybe it only has a handle on the inside so people can go out, but not come in. A safety precaution. That makes sense. And maybe it's locked.* I had a moment of panic. Maybe they button up the campus after a certain time. How would we get back in? We didn't have the phone number of the dorm and all the offices were closed. How long would we have to be missing before they came to look for us? What should we do? Bewildered, Irma put her hand on the frame. The gate swung open. We giggled and rushed through the opening. And then we got lost again.

I was no help at all finding our way back, but I didn't care. It was intoxicating. I was free. We were lost. It was dark. We were late. It didn't matter. I was having the time of my life. All of us were. None of us had ever done anything like this. Something in our eight days at GDB had made us think we could get around by ourselves. We who had felt like caged birds had made a daring flight in the night. We were giddy from adventure. We had been daring together, and now we were walking as fast as we could, trying to find the right door amidst many doors of large, dark buildings.

Finally, guided by Irma led by Chelsie, we poured through the east end door breathless and laughing, found Stephanie—"We're back!"—and rushed to our rooms to get our dogs and our dinners. I don't remember what we had that night, but it was delicious.

LOST

They had us on a basic route which we repeated every time we went out. That was so we could concentrate on skills instead of worrying about directions. We would be crossing the same streets, avoiding the same obstacles. It would be familiar. The difference was, this time I went occluded. I had put on a blindfold that let in no light at all. Scott, my O&M (orientation and mobility specialist) had warned me that the main problem partially sighted handlers had was they tended to steer their dog, not follow it. If you didn't follow your dog with complete trust, you could not graduate. So I practiced occluded with him, and chose to do today's routine route using no visual cues.

Out we went through the automatic sliding glass door straight to the curb in front of the lounge. Fourth Street. I was supposed to go left, but Hedy swerved. I corrected her and immediately lost my bearings. *Now what? Where am I? Where is Kathy?* "What should I do?" I asked.

"Figure it out," she said.

I had never done the route occluded and I was totally disoriented. "Where am I?" I asked, expecting directions. They always told me what to do. Kathy said, "Read your traffic." *What? Isn't she going to help me?* My whole life I'd been horribly nondirectional and even as an adult I was terrified of getting lost. I could still see the nightmares—I was little, swept away by the crowd. Mom couldn't find me...she never even tried...And now, in my blackness, Kathy was no longer standing nearby. Her voice was distant and it was telling me to figure it out.

Alarmed, I began to retrace in my head. *Which way did Hedy turn? What did I do after that? How far from the lounge am I? Where are the cars?*

Kathy's voice came calm and steady from my right. "Read your traffic." I took a deep breath and listened with all my might. Cars swooshed by going every which-way. I couldn't picture them. Usually I could discern surges and stops. I had good ears. I could sort them out. But there was silence and then car sounds fast and all mixed together. I couldn't tell which way they were going. "Read your traffic." Kathy's voice was even calmer and she spoke the words more slowly, as if they could come alongside and slow down my thoughts as well, but my mind was racing like a greyhound escaping through an open doorway.

I can't tell. Let me think. Hedy swerved to the left, so I am probably facing east. No, I turned back. Or did I? Where am I? What do I do? I don't know! I'm lost!

I was getting more and more confused. Finally Kathy said, "The near parallel traffic is to your right." I knew that was a huge giveaway. My brain told me I should know what that meant. It was one of the first things Scott taught me. It should have been easy to orient myself.

Fourth Street is straight out from the lounge. Oh yeah. Near parallel is to my right. No problem! But my brain was frozen.

Kathy kept saying (in that calm, even tone), "The near parallel traffic is to your right."

I couldn't breathe. Blackness was going to win. I was drowning. I stopped trying to fight. My heart said simply, *You can't do it. You failed. You should just go home.*

Maybe she saw it in my face. Maybe she just had a feeling. Her voice was different. Gentle, but firm—like a strong hand grasping my arm to pull me out of the rushing river and back to solid ground. "You have to let go of everything you thought and cut to the chase. Where are you now? Your near parallel traffic is to your right. Forget how you got there. Where are you now? Where do you want to go from here?"

Near parallel. Right. Traffic rushed by.

I still couldn't read it. I couldn't tell which direction it was going. Nothing made sense. Finally I took the blindfold off. I said, "I'm sorry. I have no idea where I am."

I was a foot from the curb directly in front of the lounge.

Feeling foolish, I put the blindfold back over my eyes. We started west on Fourth towards the corner where the music store was.

It was difficult. I didn't trust Hedy. She had been so unruly that morning that I was afraid to follow her when she swerved. Was she avoiding an obstacle or about to bury her head in a bush? Was she sniffing a passer-by or taking me around a staircase jutting out into the street? Finally Kathy stopped us. "Take off the blindfold," she said. "We need to simplify."

I was humiliated. Defeated. It wasn't as if I'd never gone occluded. Scott and I had done hours of it for just such a time as this. And yet, when it came down to the actual training, I was boggled into incoherence.

I pulled off the blindfold and looked for a place to stash it so I could hold the harness and leash. Kathy held out her hand. "I'll carry it for you." I looked up, startled at the compassion in her voice. I saw it in her face. "Sometimes you need to just focus on your dog and these," (she held up the occluders) "aren't helping you."

After that I was able to take control over Hedy using the techniques I had learned in the morning, and I loved the trip back. Hedy went past the bush with no problem and when she stopped to sniff at the place the dog had been tied in the yard, I had only to make one correction. I told Hedy to hop up and she trucked along so beautifully that it was quite enjoyable.

A few yards from the lounge, away from the hearing of others, Kathy stopped us so we could evaluate our route. What had happened at the curb? "People get concepts in their heads and they can't let go of them," she explained. "It took me a while to figure that out as an instructor. They get turned around and no matter what I say they can't understand. They've got a concept in their head and they can't let go of it. You have to be able to cut to the chase.

"Analytical people are like that. They hold onto their concept and try to figure out what went wrong. None of that matters. There's your traffic. How do you get your bearings from here? Where is my near parallel traffic and where should it be? You have to be able to leave it and move on."

I had never been able to leave anything and move on. The penalty for a repeat mistake was too high. Confucianism required strict obedience, each person fulfilling their role so society would function unhindered. It never occurred to me that I could cut to the chase, forget the failure, find my new place, and decide where to go from there. What a concept! It changed me. It was the first of many freedoms that were to follow, because of, not in spite of, the catastrophic loss of my sight.

Note: We had to complete three night routes during our time at Guide Dogs for the Blind or we could not graduate with a dog. We were released at 30-second intervals so we couldn't rely on each other. The Totals (no sight at all) and Retrains (those returning for a replacement dog) were also required to complete the route. We Regulars were new handlers, and we had never done anything like this before.

Dinner was early—5:00 p.m.—so we could do our night route at a decent hour. There was a lot of vibration in the dining room. Anxiety? Nerves? Excitement? The Totals weren't the slightest bit worried. To them it was always night. The Retrains were experienced handlers. They weren't worried either. But us Regulars—we were rather amped up. I could feel fears trying to press themselves on me, but I prayed. Instructors would be watching, hidden all over the town. What could happen?

Next to me in the bus, Stacey Ellison listened to the boisterous noises in the rear. She said, "Do you think they might be nervous?" I said we had a very loud class. Then she asked, "How do you feel about the night route, Carolyn?" I said, "I trust my dog." I surprised myself. Up till that time I hadn't realized I did.

When we got to the bus our instructors told us the route: four streets straight ahead, then make a left turn and cross two more streets to the lounge. I had trouble remembering directions and had been lost in downtown San Rafael in the daytime, so I used a technique one of the Retrains taught me. I put four kibbles in my right pocket and two in my left.

Kenny insisted on going first. He said he was very afraid. Irma said she'd be Timer and used her talking watch so she would be precise. I didn't mind waiting. Bobby was a bit apprehensive, but excited too. I stepped nearer and started singing softly, "Just a closer walk with Thee—grant it, Jesus, is my plea." Bobby joined in, "Daily walking close to Thee. Let it be, dear Lord, let it be."

Then it was his time to go. I watched Howell and him disappear into the dark.

Hedy was in her raincoat. I could see the yellow with reflective stripes, but not her head or tail. Irma helped me turn on the little flashing light that I'd fastened to Hedy's collar. Instead of my trusty black stadium coat, I was wearing a light gray GDB jacket I'd gotten at the gift shop. At least people would see us even if I couldn't see them. One by one my classmates left until Irma and I were standing there alone. She was nervous and confessed she'd wanted to be Timer and have me go last so she could pray with me before her route. We prayed for each other. Then off I went into the night.

Streets were lighted so it wasn't really too bad. Familiar landmarks were hard to see. I wasn't as sure where I was. At one point I thought I had missed a street, but it was just an extra long block. I came to the first corner. Read the traffic with my ears. Near parallel surge. "Hedy, forward." She stepped off the curb, crossed without swerving, and stopped at the up curb with her front paws on the sidewalk. "Good girl!" Kibble from the right pocket. Onward!

Shop windows were glowing with lights. Christmas colored the cool, thin air. Hedy and I passed Philip who was reworking Harlow on a clearance error, an instructor by his side. Second stop light. Another kibble. Hedy was moving fast. I was moving fast. In real life I never walked that fast. I couldn't see her—only her bright yellow coat—but I knew her head was forward, ears listening. Third crossing. Another kibble. Hedy was hauling. I couldn't remember what to do next. At the corner we passed Bobby and Howell. Instantly I knew where I was. Without realizing it, Bobby had shown me the right way to turn.

Hedy pulled steadily down Fourth Street. Now I knew where we were. There were the concrete stairs that jutted into the street. Smoothly Hedy skirted them, clearing them easily for both of us. There was the lacy orange plastic that warned pedestrians that on the other side of the barricade the sidewalk lay in pieces. Hedy cleared that too. Left pocket, one last kibble. We turned into the lounge parking lot with the glow that can only come from a fast walk in the brisk winter night with a partner you can trust.

We all arrived triumphant. I knew I had done something extraordinary. I had not walked in an unfamiliar city alone at night in forty years. The lounge was louder than usual, everyone telling how it felt to make that run. Kenny was all smiles. Debbie said when he came in with Reema he sat down on the couch with his arms around her, hugging her, tears in his eyes, exclaiming, "I love this dog! I LOVE this dog!" On the way back, Kyle and I sang in harmony. No one complained. All of us Regulars knew we had accomplished something wonderful. The night route was done swiftly and fearlessly. We had relied on our dogs and they had not let us down. We had regained our independence, our freedom. We were unstoppable. Life was good.

Eternal River

Volume III
The Next Thirty Years

Carolyn Wing Greenlee

Eternal River, Volume III, The Next Thirty Years
By Carolyn Wing Greenlee

Introduction

Many people study public records trying to trace their genealogy back through the sometimes confusing tangle of branches in their family tree. Some people say, "Oh, I have a bit of English and Irish and maybe a little Welsh," but they have no connection to those countries or understanding of the individual men and women who blended their cultures centuries before. Some merely shrug and say, "I'm Heinz 57. I'm a mutt." But me? There was never any escaping this face. My father used to tell me I had to behave better than anyone else because, if I were involved in a bank robbery with twenty others, the only one people would remember would be me. Throughout my life he'd say, "Everything you do reflects on you, our family, and all of China."

I was forty-five before I appreciated being different, and recognized the value in having a heritage that was old and deep. My parents had tried hard to instill a sense of pride in the culture and accomplishments of our race, but also made a point of living in a White neighborhood near the best schools in the country. Like so many First and Second Generation pioneers, they didn't want us to stand out; they wanted us to blend in. Assimilate. Be comfortable in an environment that was not originally our own. I tried my best to blend, and that included rejection of anything that made me unusual or "other," especially any identification with China.

Though I eagerly collected stories of earlier generations of my clan, I saw little interesting in my own life. Uncle Walter, however, was persistent, making me think in more expansive ways, prompting the family (and me personally) to write down what we remembered. The story of my journey from gagging on my grandma's handmade noodles to presenter of the Chinese American experience is included in *Eternal River, Volume III, The Next Thirty Years.* During those decades, I discovered the unique goodness of my design. At last I could establish my own place in the world—embracing my heritage, celebrating my family, enjoying the surprising blessings of friendships with unexpected people who encouraged me to pioneer my own unpredictable path through a life full of danger and opportunity.

SESQUICENTENNIAL

Carolyn: In 1998, California was celebrating the 150th anniversary of the discovery of gold in the American River. Documentaries abounded. I watched them. Most had the usual stuff but in one, the experts were women talking about women who came west, and one of the speakers said not all of them were unhappy about it. Her name was JoAnn Levy. JoAnn discovered this surprising truth as she read journals, diaries and other buried accounts, bringing them to life in a book she called "They Saw the Elephant: Women in the California Gold Rush." When asked about the meaning of the title, JoAnn explained.

JoAnn Levy: To forty-niners and those following, no expression characterized the California Gold Rush more than the words "seeing the elephant." Those planning to travel west announced they were "going to see the elephant." Those turning back claimed they had seen the "elephant's tracks" or the "elephant's tail," and confessed they'd seen more than enough of the animal. I used the phrase for my title because the expression symbolized the gold rush as an epic adventure and I wanted women to be credited for their part in it.

Carolyn: In 1998, JoAnn Levy's new book, *Daughter of Joy,* was released. This one covered another often invisible group in the west: the Chinese. On the video, JoAnn talked about them too.

I listened intently to that well-educated, insightful woman with taffy-colored hair, hearing the depth of her research and respect for the people she found. She had looked long at the subject until she knew the truth of the matter. Then she wrote accounts that

126

presented individuals who added their personalities to the chaotic mix of races, occupations, and lifestyles that colored and contoured California during the gold rush. I had never heard anyone talk about women or my people in such detail—not like a black and white group photograph of curiosities, but as portraits in full living color. JoAnn Levy became my hero. I bought *They Saw the Elephant* and read it in one gulp. Then I bought *Daughter of Joy,* and realized JoAnn knew a great deal more about my culture than I. I didn't know it was not considered shameful for a daughter to become a prostitute. My father's mother's sale to the wealthy *Gum San* woman was accepted as filial piety. She was helping her family survive. When my father told me the story of his mother's mother telling the little girl to remember their name was Dust, the dry earth trickling through her fingers, I considered it his mother's fabrication to cover her horror and humiliation—or his. JoAnn's careful research convinced me Chun Shee had done the honorable thing, and JoAnn's presentation of San Francisco courtesan Ah Toy did for me what "Thousand Pieces of Gold" had done a decade before; it changed my view of my culture, my family, and myself. I wished I could thank her in person.

I had been invited to speak at a historical society meeting in Auburn, California. Auburn's population is well aware of its variegated past, so rich in gold rush history (In the courthouse is a gold nugget as big as a computer keyboard.) and they also carry an ample awareness of the Chinese contribution to the American west. …It was fun to talk at historical gatherings to people who already knew the basics.

…After one of my presentations, someone told me I should meet Richard Yue. His aunt had given him the joss house that the family owned. Recently, he unlocked the door for the first time in twenty years. Except for papers thrown about by intruders looking for valuables, it was exactly as it had been when the last "bachelor" Chinese man left in the 1970s. I called Richard and set up a time to meet him at the Gold Rush Days sesquicentennial celebration that was taking place the next day.

That night I scanned the newspaper to see what was scheduled, and there among the speakers was a name I did not expect to see: JoAnn Levy. My hero! Wow! If I had known she was going to be there, I would have brought my copies of her books. I decided to buy one there so she could sign it for me, and started rehearsing what I would say when I met her.

The Gold Country Fairground was large and packed with exhibits, demonstrations, food, tourists, and a stage coach robbery ever so often. Where was JoAnn Levy? I searched through the tent city, past vendors, musicians, and craftsmen, trying my best not to run over any small children. I rounded a far corner, and there, seated at a little table with neatly stacked books, was a lovely woman with taffy-colored hair.

Forgetting my carefully crafted introduction, I rushed up blurting, "You're my hero!" JoAnn looked a little startled. "No one has ever said that to me before," she replied with a smile. I tried to tell her what she had done for me, not just the research but the way she regarded the people she wrote about—especially women and the Chinese. I was rushing because I didn't want to monopolize her time, and that made it worse. I felt foolish. I was talking to my hero and I was incoherent. I told her I had brought her a present and gave her a copy of my mom's book. Then I told her I wanted to buy a copy of *Daughter of Joy* and asked her to sign it for me. She smiled and wrote "To Kathleen Kong Wing." "Oh," I interrupted. "That's my mother. I'm Carolyn."

JoAnn was appalled. She had looked at the names on the cover and assumed the first one listed was mine. I assured her I didn't care. I was just happy to meet her and have a chance to tell her what her talk and books had meant to me.

Still dismayed, JoAnn was staring at her handwriting, wondering what to do. Then she quickly added to the inscription. Now it read, "To Carolyn and to Kathleen Kong Wing, I know you will applaud with me the extraordinary courage of this remarkable woman. Thank you for caring that I did this."

We agreed it was perfect.

I know published writers are humans like everyone else. I've been one myself for twenty years. I've also been to book signings where the author treated her adoring fans like nuisances, and refused to write more than her name on the page. Those writers make it clear they are not there to chat, or even hear how their books touched our hearts.

I've never forgotten how gracious JoAnn was that day—how she accepted my words—and me—with warmth. She was generous with her time, listening carefully, receiving my praise (not an easy thing to do well), and the attention she gave me was genuine. I have done quite a few talks and book signings since. Afterwards there are sometimes long lines of people who want to talk to me. I give each one my full attention. Even if it can't be for very long, they deserve my respect. I learned from JoAnn.

The Other Forty-niners

Carolyn: With ill-contained excitement I attended JoAnn Levy's presentation at the Auburn Fairground, arriving early for a front row seat. A couple of hours later I went back for the second presentation even though it was the same talk. I reveled in every story deftly sketched. The historical records she'd found astonished me. Some law officers stood up for Chinese who had been ousted by claim jumpers. There was a judge who awarded damages to Ah Toy, a Chinese woman, even though she was a courtesan.

JoAnn was fair. She didn't lionize anyone. She made no one a villain. To her, each human being was an individual with a voice and a story worth remembering, not just the miners. There were many other intriguing individuals peopling the gold rush and she found them by digging. What she brought to life was more precious than a gold nugget as big as a computer keyboard.

JoAnn Levy: The presence of tens of thousands of Chinese in California during the gold rush is too often overlooked. Their contributions of the state's culture and economy deserve recognition and appreciation. They came for gold like all the adventurers, but they stayed to build an agricultural wonderland, construct levees, hurl a railroad over a mountain.

And the several thousand of women who, through choice, chance, or circumstance, found themselves in California during the 'great adventure' have been equally ignored in favor of that red-shirted miner in the slouch hat, a pick on his shoulder. After the gold fever subsided, many of those overlooked women remained to help settle the land.

Although they are today a neglected part of gold rush history, the "other" forty-niners—the women in sunbonnets and the Chinese in basket hats among them—were here when history was being made. And they helped make it.

Westward Women

Introduction

When my husband was scheduled to teach at a chiropractic college in St. Louis, we took the opportunity to make the long journey in an ancient motorhome, tracing the Lewis and Clark route in reverse to Missouri, then following the Oregon/California Trail back to California. We had picked out multiple museums and historical sites to visit, and we wanted to see for ourselves what it was like to feel the hot, relentless winds across the flatlands and walk in the shadows of the towering white rocks of Scotts Bluff.

Before we left I was working on a poem about the changes in women as they journeyed west, but I couldn't get the ending. However, after experiencing many of the hardships that characterized that journey, I knew exactly what to write. It wasn't about change, adjustment, or adaptation to a new way of life; it was transformation.

WESTWARD WOMEN

Westward women
    weren't always willing
    but love
    or fear
        pressed them to beginning
        from the spot called
            "Independence"

Westward women
    weren't the same when they arrived
    as the ones they started out
    as the ones they left behind

Westward women
    buried husbands under trees
    left their china in the dust
        by castoff wheels
        broken by ruts
            by jostling and pounding
                by parch
                by scorch
                by snow
                    drifted high and holy white
                        covering cattle
                        standing hollow
                        covering bellows
                        growing weaker
                        old and younger
                        growing weaker

                hunger held them helpless
            and boredom trudging step by step
        counting dangers
    two thousand miles

    Westward Woman
        figured out
            how to fix a dandy meal

131

over buffalo dung
they selected themselves
no longer worried
about spoiling their hands
tried to describe
with words too small
what only Overlanders saw
spire stones
prairie dogs
yellow orange lace
under water smelling foul
prairies so flat
nothing stopped the wind
mountainsides so sheer
they broke your heart just to look

Westward Woman
made love
babies
home on the range
rinsed their dried red rags
discreetly
(when there was water)
kept their woman-hearts
discarded all the rest

When Westward women arrived
they had learned to improvise
set up new lives
in split skirts
riding astride
knew they were strong
could do a man's work and
not be one
having
driven cattle
battled bugs and varmints
scuttling in darkness
and snakes

Westward women
> couldn't wonder anymore
> what folks back home would think—
> they had become
> Women of the West
> and couldn't explain
> or have to.

What Do You Remember?

"I thought you'd be interested in this." Uncle Bill handed me a paper. "I think you can use it." It was a letter from Uncle Walter to his siblings, dated July 27, 1974.

Dear Family,

A week ago Lai and I came across this photograph of "Pop", and I decided each of you would want a copy. I believe the newspaper story describes the occasion as a visit by Dr. Sun Yat-Sen (second row, center) with his followers. The year is 1911. The place is St. Mary's, San Francisco Chinatown. The circled numbers label the five members from our Chinese village.

At this time Pop was 23 years old, living in S.F. away from his family. Four years earlier he had gone back to China to marry his picture bride. There his first son was born (Lai). It would be four years after the photograph before Mom and Lai would get their papers to join him in the U.S. When his family arrived, after one year in S.F., they settled in Merced, starting a Chinese hand laundry. There in the small town were born Bill, Kathleen, Walter, Marilyn and Katie. And there the family grew up together, until the marriages of the children and the deaths of Pop and Mom.

What do you remember of those early days?

133

1. I remember how Pop and Mom talked for hours each day, while he ironed the white shirts next to Mom who ironed the colored shirts. Their enthusiasm for news was especially great during the Japanese invasion of China in the 1930's. Pop would avidly read the "Young Republic" Chinese newspaper to Mom, then both would ask me to interpret what the S.F. "Examiner" said about the events in China. "China's long-swordsmen in furious hand-to-hand combat have defeated the Japanese and their mechanized machine-guns at Canton," he would elate. "General Chiang Kai-Shek will never compromise China's unity and complete victory!" This new photograph gives me a deeper perspective of why Pop showed such a strong Chinese nationalistic spirit in a U.S. Chinese laundry.

2. I remember Pop regularly sending back to his village part of the money earned from the laundry. The money was designated for the education of his younger brother's oldest son, Dick, who was to go to Nanking University. Then as principal in the village school, Cousin Dick would help provide an education for the people in the village. Pop also talked fondly of returning to China and encouraged me to complete my education at Stanford and use it to help electrify the village with its first lighting system. "It would be wonderful," he said, "if there were lights at night in the homes." But the Communists took over the village in 1951, and after that Pop gradually gave up hope for the China he cherished, and finally accepted the fate of dying in a strange land. This new photograph helps explain to me how a Chinese hand-laundryman lived such high ideals. As a boy I felt the lowness of an illiterate laundryman's social status. I couldn't see the makings of my father, and only today, long after his death, do I see the beauty and range of his life.

3. I remember Pop getting up at 5:30 each morning to start the washing machine--adjusting the boiler, putting in the soap,

and operating the wringer. When I am near the roaring waters of a river, the sounds and the water often remind me of Pop's washing machine. "Hey, Pop is washing clothes," I have said to myself several times. On this summer's vacation at Butte, Montana, we came upon an historical museum that displayed a washing machine run by belts like the one I remember. We took pictures of it. The memories come back. I was a little boy crawling under the washing machine to search again among the buttons for small coins sifted out by the tumbling. And there was Pop applying wax to the belts to keep them from slipping. And I wondered again, as I did so many times when I was a little boy, "How could Pop get up so early before I awoke, and work so late, after I went to sleep?" Mom always showed us concern and love in a demonstrative way, but it took me much longer to understand the kind of love Pop showed us. Today's photograph reminds me of a 5:30 father who toiled unceasingly. Will I ever perceive the nobility of his life?

4. I remember when Pop used to take me to S.F. on the Greyhound bus. We would cross the Ferry, ride the Market Street-car, transfer to the Geary car to the Zoo, and after a full day, we would return to Merced, arriving about 9:00 p.m. when everyone would be waiting to visit, while we cooked and ate large amounts of fresh noodles Pop had bought in the City. As I look today at his photograph, I wonder if he enjoyed going to the City with me as much as I enjoyed the vacation trips I have taken with Gerrit, Brian and Marguerite? Or did he have a greater capacity to be a father than I?

5. I remember how Pop cooked salmon heads with tomatoes. He liked crackers in peanut oil and tea. Our family drank kettles of diluted lemon juice and large amounts of rice juk. By China's village standards, our living conditions were normal. Only by today's new standards of suburban Palo Alto were we "poor". It's strange how unimportant material things become as we grow older. On this year's vacation to a fine restaurant in Vancouver Chinatown, I ordered a luxurious dinner. One of the dishes was a large whole fish elegantly cooked and carved at the table. If I could have had a

choice, I would have wished it had been salmon heads and toma-toes plus the memory of Pop.

6. I remember dropping a Chinese iron on Katie's head. She still has that scar today. The iron, heated on a coal fire, was picked up and held by an insulated pad. I think the iron I hit Katie's head with was only lukewarm. I wouldn't think of hitting my sister with a hot iron. Anyway, she screamed louder than I thought she would, as part of the protection of a younger sister. So I ran out of the house. Up to this time, Pop had never chased me. But this crime in his eyes was so dastard that he went tearing out of the front door after me. To this day I'll never know how he caught me. I had always visualized him as ironing and washing. I never thought he could also run. He cornered me behind the blacksmith shop, and pulled me screaming by my ears. (I remember now that Chinese parents used to discipline their children by hitting their heads with chopsticks or twisting their ears. Not only does it hurt, but it is supposed to bring shame to the children.) Pop took me to the backyard chicken-house and switched me with the bamboo tongs he gathered from the rice sacks. This was another surprise. He had never used bamboo tongs before. I guess he thought the punishment demanded more than chopsticks or ear twisting. I remember yelling for all posterity. Only once was I ever "spanked" by Pop. It was enough to learn that some things can not (sic) be negotiated--like dropping irons on people's head and saying sorry.

7. I remember Pop grinding hamburger and cutting up stew. That was one of his main jobs at the market after he sold the laundry. He would start each day bringing the cash for the register; then he swept the floor and wiped the meat counter. In the back room, he boned the meat and scraps for hamburger and stew. This was the least skillful and usually least preferred job in the market. He could have been the "boss" or supervisor-owner, but he chose to work diligently wherever he could. Not able to speak English, all his life he relegated himself to the humble conditions of the laundry and meat market. For a long time during my youth, be-

cause my eyes were mainly of the world, I could not see Pop's greatness. This vacation we have talked much about the meaning of service to others. When I struggled to decide how much of my time I should strive to serve others, I realized that Pop had totally served others as an everyday natural way of life. When I sought prestigious and professional ways for service, I recalled that Pop found service in the unskilled and menial chores. When I searched the world literature and scriptures for the meaning of love, I found the concrete example in the life of my father. When he died, I thought of only one person. His dedicated life reminded me of the humble carpenter of Nazareth who washed his disciple's feet.

I know each of you have stories or incidents you re- member about Pop, Mom and the family during the early years. Will you please write them down in brief as if you were talking to each of us. Send them to me and I will type and circulate them to others in the family. My best regards to each of you this day and always.
—Walter

It was 1999 when I read Uncle Walter's letter, and the Second Generation was already getting frail. Uncle Walter himself was suffering from diabetes. He no longer had the energy or vision necessary to type stories, let alone coax them out of his siblings. I realized that, through the interviews I had conducted during our three Gong reunions at *Ching Ming,* I had taken up Uncle Walter's charge without being asked, collecting and writing the stories of a clan that was started by two illiterate Chinese who came here on false papers because, back home, people were eating the bark off the trees.

WILDFLOWER SEASON

We are wildflowers,
  scattered,
      wind sown
Warm rich meadows are our homes,
ice regions of the North,
sand-washed sullen hot breath plains,
cracks of rocks
  cheerful cascadings
      celebrating roots that hold

We are often
  individually
  unseen
We have beauties known
  mostly to ourselves
We have learned to live
  where greenhouse flowers die,
     We who are vapor ourselves
  From the window of a passing car,
  we are massing
     all alike
     an array of force and color
     covering the world
From where we sit,
we are each ourselves
     separate,
     but close
     opening and closing
     alone.

We bring delight with variety,
tears
  with the soft yellow dust of our fertility
We are opulent, lush, generous
          gone

trusting the rest to integrity of seeds
and the faithfulness of tomorrow